The Scooter

The
Scooter
The Phil Rizzuto Story

Gene Schoor

Charles Scribner's Sons New York

For Terry Shore, Lisa Grace,

and all the crowd at

Martin Van Buren High School,

Queens Village, N.Y.

Photo credits: Frontispiece, The National
Baseball Hall of Fame and Museum, Inc.;
insert, p. C (top), UPI; p. C (bottom),
Wide World Photos; p. E, UPI.

Library of Congress Cataloging in Publication Data
Schoor, Gene.
The Scooter: The Phil Rizzuto story.
Includes index.
1. Rizzuto, Phil, 1918–   2. Baseball
players—United States—Biography.   3. New York
Yankees (Baseball team)   I. Title.
GV865.R5S36   1982   796.357′092′4   [B]   82–10264
ISBN 0–684–17635–1

1 3 5 7 9 11 13 15 17 19   F/C   20 18 16 14 12 10 8 6 4 2

Printed in the United States of America.

Contents

A selection of photographs follows page 132.

1

"Get Yourself
a Shoeshine Box!"

Dominick Angotti was a bit tense, nervous. So was the young nephew he was driving to Ebbets Field in Brooklyn. Ebbets Field was the bandbox home of the Brooklyn Dodgers in 1935. Dom and his nephew had been in the ballpark often enough, watching the Bums, as they were affectionately called in Flatbush and all points east. Both of them were rabid Dodger fans. Everybody in Brooklyn—Long Island, too—was a Dodger fan in those days. But on this trip they weren't just going to see a game.

"We'll be there in a few minutes," said Uncle Dom.

"Sure," said his nephew.

For a moment there was silence between them. The young nephew looked out on the traffic moving up and down Flatbush Avenue, but his mind was on the diamond in the field he knew so well.

"You're feeling all right?" asked his uncle.

"I'm feeling great," said the young star.

"Just keep cool," said Uncle Dominick. "Keep your eye on the ball."

"Don't worry about me. This isn't the first time I'm going to be playing ball," he snapped.

"All right, all right," protested Uncle Dominick. "You don't have to bite my head off."

"Sorry, Uncle."

The young fellow smiled. He had an engaging smile.

"I guess I'm just a little nervous. Sorry."

He had reason to be nervous. Sixteen years old, just a bit over five feet tall in his cleated shoes, weighing about 130 pounds soaking wet, he was on his way to show Casey Stengel, manager of the Brooklyn Dodgers, that he, Phil Rizzuto, was good enough to play professional baseball. It was enough to put butterflies in anyone's stomach.

There wasn't a kid in Brooklyn or near it who hadn't been possessed by dreams of glory, of making that impossible play in the infield and turning it into a game-saving double play, of hitting the ball for an inside-the-park home run and sliding under the tag at the plate with the game-winning run. Phil lived in Glendale, just over the Brooklyn border in Long Island, but he had been born in Brooklyn and was a die-hard Dodger fan.

"I'm going to make it, Uncle," he said as he changed from his street shoes into his spikes and the adrenaline began to flow. "Watch me go!"

"Go, Phil! Go!" shouted Uncle Dom as he watched his young nephew trot out onto the sacred soil of Ebbets Field.

There were about 150 young guys on the field, all invited for the tryouts, but Uncle Dom had eyes only for his young nephew.

Phil looked around for Casey Stengel but couldn't see him. Casey wasn't anywhere in the park. Phil would have recognized him; anyone in or around baseball would have recognized the legendary Casey, if he had been there.

Phil was disappointed, but he didn't have time to think about why Casey wasn't around. Otto Miller and Zach Taylor, two of Casey's coaches, were getting all the would-be ballplayers out into left-center field, lining them up, dividing them into groups of twenty.

"When I say, 'Go,' I want you to race for the first base stripe," barked Otto Miller, "and I mean race!"

Zach Taylor walked over to the first base line and signaled Miller to get things going.

"Go!" snapped Miller, and the first twenty kids raced for the finish line.

"You! You! You! You! You!" said Zach Taylor, pointing to the first five who had crossed the line. "Stick around!"

He looked at the fifteen losers. "Sorry, boys," he said. "You can pack up and go home. Maybe you can try again next year."

He signaled Miller for the next twenty, and the ritual was repeated. Five of the hopefuls were told to stick around. Fifteen more were sent home. They weren't fast enough for the Dodgers' coaches.

Mel Ott, who played for the New York Giants when he was only seventeen years old, about the age of most of the youngsters running for Miller and Taylor that afternoon, would have been sent home by the coaches, too. He just wasn't fast on his feet. Nor were other players who made it to the big leagues, all-time greats such as Lou Gehrig, Ted Williams, Jimmy Foxx, and Babe Ruth!

Young Phil Rizzuto was in the third group of twenty. He wasn't worried by what he saw happening along the first base line. He knew he could outrun anyone on the field that day.

"Go!" snapped Miller, and Phil Rizzuto never ran faster in

all his life. He was across the finish line yards in front of the fellows behind him.

He smiled up at his uncle in the stands. He had passed his first test. He could already see himself playing alongside Joe Stripp, Tony Cuccinello, Lonny Frey, Frenchy Bordagaray, and Al Lopez, all Dodger heroes in 1935.

There were only forty kids left in the park, after the races were run. The coaches divided them into two groups. One group went into the field, the other was to show what it could do with the bat. Phil Rizzuto was in the second group.

Even at sixteen, Phil knew that he was better in the field than he was with the bat, but he wasn't worried too much as he picked up a bat and assumed his stance at the plate. After all, he had been a good hitter when he played for his high school team, and he had been better than a so-so hitter on his semipro team, playing with guys who were much bigger, much heavier, and much older than he was. Nervous? A little. But that was natural enough. Confident? Certainly! He knew he was going to hit that ball, and hit it where the fielders couldn't touch it.

Phil looked out at the big right-hander on the mound, a kid like himself, trying to impress the Dodger coaches.

He tapped home plate with his bat, swung it menacingly a couple of times, cocked it as the young pitcher went into his windup and let the ball go.

But the kid pitcher was wild. It didn't take more than the fraction of a second for Phil to see that the pitch was off the plate, inside. He raised his bat and turned to avoid the ball, but the kid pitcher was fast and the ball hit Phil square in the back, sending him sprawling into the dust.

Phil was in pain. He was winded. He should have walked

out of the batter's box after he got to his feet. He should have rested for a while before stepping up to the plate again. He certainly should have waited until the pain in his back had subsided. But instinctively he knew that he had to get back into the box fast, that coach Otto Miller would have just sent him home with the other losers if he took any time at all. Above all, he didn't want Miller to think that he was afraid, scared of a close pitch, worried about being hit by the ball.

There never had been any doubt about Phil Rizzuto's courage, but this time he paid for that courage. The kid pitcher found the plate but Phil was in such pain that he could hardly swing his bat.

He waved weakly at a couple of pitches, and that was all, missing balls he would ordinarily have sent screaming through the infield.

"Okay, sonny," said Otto Miller. "That's it. Sorry, but you're not ready yet, little fellow." Then, almost as an after-thought, "It's a good thing that big guy didn't hurt you."

Young sixteen-year-old Phil Rizzuto fought to keep back the tears.

It was a tough break. Another pitcher, or if the ball had been over the plate, and it might have been a different story. There might have been a different story for the Brooklyn Dodgers, too.

Years later, Casey Stengel would be embarrassed by how the Dodgers had sent Phil Rizzuto home, failing to recognize the great potential of the young ballplayer. Somehow it got around that Casey was responsible for letting Phil get away. But Casey wasn't in the ballpark that day. Stengel had a sharp eye for talent, and if he had been at Ebbets Field that day in 1935, he certainly would have tried young Rizzuto out in the field, as well as at bat. He wouldn't have let Phil go that easily, and Rizzuto might have made history in Ebbets Field.

"They didn't give you much of a tryout," said Uncle Dominick. "What did they expect you to do after that kid nearly killed you? No wonder they're in seventh place."

Phil wasn't easily consoled.

"I didn't make it," he said. "That's all. I didn't make it."

"What do you mean you didn't make it?" Uncle Dom shouted. He was no less disappointed than his nephew, but he was even more angry than disappointed. "They didn't give you a chance! They'll be sorry! Just you wait and see! There are other baseball teams! You'll come back to stick it to those Bums!"

Uncle Dom was right in more ways than one. The revenge would come with time. Tryouts with other baseball teams would come even quicker. It was only a couple of weeks after that disappointing episode in Ebbets Field that Phil got a letter from the New York Giants, asking him to come up to the Polo Grounds, the Giants' ballpark, for a tryout.

Again it was Uncle Dominick who drove young Phil to the Giants' bailiwick.

"Didn't I tell you there were other ball teams?" he gloated. "Now you go out there and show them!"

Phil may not have been as confident in the bigger ballpark as he was at Ebbets Field, but he was glad to see that there were only about fifty kids assembled for the tryouts. This would mean more time to show off his ability, how he could hit, run, play shortstop. And that is exactly what the management of the New York Giants intended. Unfortunately for Phil, and for the Giants, Rizzuto never got the chance to demonstrate his great potential.

Bill Terry, another all-time baseball great, was managing the Giants in 1935, but, like Stengel, he was not in the ballpark the day young Rizzuto was to try out. Frank (Pancho) Snyder, one of Terry's coaches, was in charge of the field that day.

Pancho Snyder was a big man. He was built like a truck. A man had to be big to impress him at all. And Pancho Snyder was tough, hard-boiled.

He took one look at the sixteen-year-old, five-foot, 130-pound Phil Rizzuto and, before the youngster could so much as pick up a ball, practically blew him out of the Polo Grounds.

"You're too small, kid," he snarled. "What makes you think you can play ball? Go home and get yourself a shoe-shine box!"

Phil was too paralyzed to answer, to protest, to even ask for a chance. He stood there for a moment, as if transfixed. There were no tears in his eyes this time. He just couldn't believe what he had heard. Phil had always been a rather mild fellow, not given to argument; he still is that way. After a moment, he just turned, walked off the field, and joined his waiting uncle.

"What happened?" asked Dominick, startled. "What are you doing here? Why aren't you down there, showing them what you can do?"

"You wouldn't believe me if I told you," said Phil. "Let's go home."

Get yourself a shoeshine box.

Get a shoeshine box indeed! Anyone else might have been thoroughly discouraged, hung up his glove, and burned his uniform. Not Phil Rizzuto. Young Phil Rizzuto had heart. He was ambitious. He had one dream in life: he was going to play professional baseball and he was going to be a good professional ballplayer, the best. Ebbets Field and the Polo Grounds could dismiss him, send him off for a shoeshine box, but he would show them the stuff he was made of, make them regret the offhand manner in which they had treated him, he promised himself. And that was certainly one promise he was to keep.

2

A Cricket
in the Outfield

The Rizzutos and the Angottis came to this country before the turn of the century. They settled in the downtown section of Brooklyn a short distance from the Brooklyn Bridge. It was an area already peopled with a good number of immigrants from Italy. New York was, and still is to a great extent, an amalgamation of ethnic enclaves, each enclave a Little Poland, a Little Hungary, a Little Ireland, a Little Italy. Coming to a new land, the immigrants felt more secure with others who had come from the same country in Europe, spoke the same language, observed the same customs. It was in this Little Italy near the Brooklyn Bridge that Philip Rizzuto and Rose Angotti were born. It was here, too, that the first American-born Philip Rizzuto met and fell in love with Rose Angotti and, in 1913, married her.

1913 wasn't a very good year. The country was going through one of its periodic economic recessions. Jobs were scarce and money scarcer, but Philip Rizzuto managed to get himself a job as a day laborer, a ditch digger, a road worker. The pay wasn't great but the Rizzutos had a roof over their heads and they didn't go hungry.

A year after they were married, there was an addition to the

9

family, a daughter, named Mary. Two years later, in 1916, there was another child, another daughter. The Rizzutos named her Rose, after her mother.

With two more mouths to feed in the family, Rizzuto began to look around for a job that would bring home a steady income. Day-laboring was just too uncertain. There were too many days when there was no work at all or when the weather didn't permit any work to be done. With a bit of luck Rizzuto found himself a job with the Brooklyn Rapid Transit Company, as a trolley car conductor. There aren't any more trolley cars in New York today, having been replaced by buses years ago. But back in 1917, when Rizzuto got his job, trolley cars, running on tracks, with wires overhead, cut through and connected every part of the city.

It wasn't an easy job, being a conductor on a trolley, particularly in 1917. There was no Transport Workers Union then, and the men who worked the trolleys put in ten, twelve, and fourteen hours a day. The pay wasn't too good either, but the pay envelope arrived regularly, and that was enough at the time for Philip Rizzuto.

The trolley to which he was assigned ran from Ridgewood to Richmond Hill, from Brooklyn to the borough of Queens, and back again. To make things just a bit easier for himself and his family, Rizzuto found a small frame house on Dill Place in Ridgewood. Dill Place was a nondescript little street. The house was small, its entrance in a tiny alleyway. But it was the best that Philip Rizzuto's income would allow. It was on Dill Place in Ridgewood that Rose Rizzuto gave birth to her third child, a son, on September 25, 1918. They named the boy after his father, Philip Francis Rizzuto, Jr. One more son, Alfred, came two years later.

When everyone around you is poor, you don't understand the meaning of poverty. Mama Rizzuto had to pinch the pennies Papa Rizzuto brought home every week, but the family didn't go hungry. There was always plenty of food on the table, a bottle of wine for Papa. There were family dinners, birthday parties, other celebrations. There was even an occasional Saturday afternoon movie. The kids didn't feel deprived or underprivileged.

They went to the local school, Public School 68, in Ridgewood. Every Sunday they went to church. The Rizzutos were a religious family. There was no missing church on Sunday.

Once in a while, Phil Jr. was given the privilege of taking lunch to his father. Papa couldn't come home for lunch, and eating out was more than the family budget could afford.

"Here's Papa's lunch," Mama would say, handing Phil the tin lunch box, adding, as always, "Be careful."

"I'll be careful," Phil said, and off he went to meet the trolley his father rode from Brooklyn to Queens and back again.

He waited at the appointed corner. He strained his eyes looking to see whether the trolley car was coming or not, strained his ears for the sound of it. He stepped on the tracks. When the tracks began to vibrate, he knew his father was near.

Actually, the trolley cars made an awful racket, and it wasn't difficult to know how near or far away one was. It was all a game for young Phil, and he liked nothing better than a game. Waiting at the corner was a game. Waiting for the trolley to come was a game. Climbing on to the trolley, giving his father his lunch, was a game. Riding a few blocks on the trolley, as his father opened his lunch box and examined its contents, was a game, too.

But the game Phil liked best was baseball. The Rizzuto boys

played ball twelve months a year. There was stickball, softball, touch football, but best of all—baseball.

"Ball, ball, ball," said his mother. "Don't you ever think of anything else?"

The truth is that little else occupied young Phil's mind, and, in fact, he had been conditioned, almost from infancy, to think of nothing but baseball.

When he was only four years old, his father gave him a bat and a glove. His mother sewed up his first baseball uniform when he was only eight. And all the talk in the house, especially when Uncle Dominick was around, was about baseball, and particularly about the Dodgers.

The New York Giants were the enemy. The New York Yankees were in another league—another country to Dodger fans—and, as such, were foreigners. But old-time heroes of the Brooklyn Dodgers—Sherrod Smith, Babe Herman, Burleigh Grimes, Dazzy Vance, Zach Wheat, and others—were household names in the Rizzuto family. At supper time the kids and Mama could talk all they wanted when the news came on the radio. But as soon as the sportscaster came on, Papa would command, "Hush!" And a total, almost reverent silence fell over the table as Papa listened to the results of the day's baseball games. Phil and his brother Al listened, too.

"Phil was the smallest boy in the games," said Mrs. Rizzuto, who couldn't help being a fan herself, "but he ran faster than anyone else."

She wished he would grow a bit taller, but she was proud enough of his speed.

"When Phil had to run, he would run so fast that there wasn't anyone who could catch him, not even the biggest of the boys."

Phil was a bit self-conscious about his size, but he made up for it by his speed, his sheer determination, and his great natural ability. He was always playing somewhere in a baseball game with guys who were older and certainly bigger than he was.

There was no baseball team in the public school he attended, but there were a number of sandlot teams in the neighborhood—teams organized by such organizations as the Police Athletic League and the Elks Club—and that's where Phil did most of his playing. And as often as not he came home after a game with his hands and face scratched and bruised and his uniform torn and tattered.

"Look at you, will you!" yelled Mama. "How am I going to fix that suit? And you look like you've been in a fight again! Come here! Let me clean the blood off your face! Where's the iodine?"

"It's all right, Mama," Phil would protest. "I'm not hurt. We cleaned up the lot, but I guess we left some rocks and some glass around. I tell you I'm all right, Mama, but maybe you can sew up some of these rips in the uniform."

Mama helped clean up his face and hands, over his protests. She complained about all the rips in his uniform, but she sewed them up. And Phil was ready for his next adventure with the perils and pitfalls of sandlot baseball.

When Phil reached the ripe age of nine, there was a change in the fortunes of the Rizzuto family. It was 1927 and the country was living in one of the more prosperous eras of its history. No one spoke of unemployment. Everybody was working and making all sorts of money—everybody but Papa Rizzuto, who was pulling down forty dollars a week, working for the trolley lines. Papa decided it was time to make a move, to trade in his conductor uniform and make some real money. He quit his job and went to work for a construction company, building houses. Everybody and his cousin was making a small down payment, buying a newly built house. The era of prosperity was to come to an abrupt halt in only a couple of years, but nobody had that in mind, or expected it, in the halcyon days of 1927.

With Papa's new job and bigger paycheck, the Rizzutos began to put some money in the bank. Soon there was enough money to make a down payment on a new house.

"We need to live in a nicer place, Phil," said Mama. "The girls are growing up. There'll be boy friends. They should come to a nice house. They shouldn't have to walk through a dirty little alley to come to the front door."

Mr. Willenbucher, a real estate agent, sold the Rizzutos a house on a corner lot in Glendale. It was a two-family stucco house. The Rizzutos took the ground floor for themselves and fixed up the cellar so the two boys, Phil and Alfred, could sleep in it; they rented the upstairs apartment to help pay the mortgage and the real estate taxes.

The Rizzuto family took possession of their house early in 1930. It might have been an occasion for much celebration and much joy. It wasn't. In October of 1929, the Wall Street stock market crashed. People who had invested millions went broke. So did thousands of little people who lost their life savings as the prices on the stock market came tumbling down.

Herbert Hoover, then president of the United States, declared that the economy of the country was in great shape. So did any number of bankers and industrialists. The truth was that the country was just beginning the greatest depression in its history. There would be millions unemployed, bread lines, soup lines, shanty towns called Hoovervilles that would provide the only shelter many, far too many, could find. There would be countless men at countless corners, selling apples, trying every possible way to earn enough to feed themselves and their families.

Philip Rizzuto lost his lucrative job with the construction company. Nobody was building any new houses. He managed to get his old job back, with Brooklyn Rapid Transit, but he had lost the ten years of seniority he had accumulated. He returned to work as a conductor on a part-time basis. He was paid when they had work for him. When there was no work, there was no paycheck either.

Life was hard for the Rizzutos in those days, as hard as it was for hundreds of thousands of people in the United States. Philip Rizzuto, who had never asked for a handout in his life, was suddenly forced to swallow his pride and apply for home relief, social welfare. Mrs. Rizzuto took in sewing to help meet the family needs. Young Phil pitched in and added a few pennies to the family income by delivering papers.

Times were tough, but the Rizzutos were tough, too. They managed through good times; they would manage through bad times; and Phil Rizzuto would keep playing ball.

He was twelve years old and he was playing ball with boys who were fifteen and sixteen, as good as some and better than most. He was only four feet tall but he could hit, he could catch any ball in the outfield, and he was the fastest runner on the team.

His first team went by the name of the Ridgewood Robins. The Robins is what the Brooklyn Dodgers were called for a period, in honor of the legendary Hall of Famer Wilbert (Uncle Robbie) Robinson, who managed the team from 1914 to 1931.

The manager of the Ridgewood team was Mr. Willenbucher,

the same Mr. Willenbucher who had sold the Rizzutos their house in Glendale.

"What do you play?" Willenbucher asked the diminutive Rizzuto, the first time the kid asked to join the team.

"I'm an outfielder," said young Phil, as if he were a veteran of the baseball wars.

Willenbucher looked down at the youngster. There was a twinkle in his eye. Most kids think they're as good as any big fellow in the game.

"I can see how you can cover the outfield," said Willenbucher. "You're a cricket!"

If Phil was embarrassed, he didn't show it.

"Yeah, Mr. Willenbucher," he said. "I can cover the outfield."

The regulars of the Ridgewood Robins were less kind.

"What are you going to do, Mr. Willenbucher? Play midgets on the team?"

"He's a little runt, Mr. Willenbucher."

"Shrimp!"

Young Phil smiled and shrugged off the insults. He didn't care what they called him, so long as he could get onto the field and play.

"You really want to play?" asked a still-unbelieving Willenbucher.

"Yeah. I want to play," said Phil.

"OK," said the coach. "Let's see what you've got."

They sent him up to the plate and he hit one pitch after another, solid hits all. They put him out in the field, and he did cover the outfield a little like a cricket, only faster.

"You're all right," said Mr. Willenbucher. His teammates agreed.

The kids still called him "Midget" and "Runt" and

"Shrimp," but they knew they had a good little player on their team, and it was with affection, not ridicule, that they teased the youngster.

Phil played his first game in a major league park with the Ridgewood Robins. The Robins got there by winning every game they played in a sandlot tournament that was sponsored by the now-defunct Brooklyn newspaper, the *Standard Union*. There was just one more game to win, against the Coney Island Athletics, and they would be crowned the sandlot champions of Brooklyn. That final game was to be played in Ebbets Field, home of the Brooklyn Dodgers.

At game time, Phil Rizzuto was as excited as anyone else on the Ridgewood Robins, but Mr. Willenbucher cooled him down.

"Look here, Phil," he said, taking the kid aside. "You want the team to win, don't you?"

"Sure!" That was an odd question, thought Phil.

"You'll do what I tell you then?" queried the manager.

"Sure! Sure!" said Phil. He didn't know what Mr. Willenbucher had in mind, but he knew that a ballplayer followed the skipper's orders.

"OK," said Mr. Willenbucher. "Every time you get up to bat, you just stand there."

"Just stand there?" asked the puzzled youngster.

"Yeah. Just stand there. Don't swing your bat. Whatever they pitch you, just take it."

Young Phil didn't understand.

"See," explained the manager, "you're only four feet tall. They can't possibly pitch to you. Every time you get up, they'll walk you. We need men on base to win the game, kid. Don't you see?"

Phil nodded his head. There was a lump in his throat and he

couldn't talk. Sure he was small, and maybe he would get a walk every time he came to the plate, but here he was in a dream of glory, playing ball in Ebbets Field, and the skipper wasn't going to let him swing the bat.

His first time at the plate, Phil followed orders. He scarcely lifted the bat from his shoulder and sure enough, as Mr. Willenbucher had predicted, he got his base on balls.

That made him feel a little better. The pitcher hadn't come anywhere near the strike zone, and he wouldn't have reached for a bad pitch in any case.

The first time he took the field, the biggest outfield he'd ever played, Phil felt kind of lost; there was so much space and it seemed to him he was miles away from the other Ridgewood outfielders. But in spite of his diminutive size, Phil played the outfield well. He had no trouble with the fly balls that came his way. There was no error chalked up against him in that championship game. He did so well in the field that he began to chafe at his orders not to swing at the ball.

Nevertheless, he did follow orders. He'd go up right-handed one time, left-handed the next, just to cut the monotony at the plate. And right-handed or left-handed, the first four times he came to bat, he was walked.

The fifth time was another story. The Coney Islander pitcher this time found Phil's range and whipped two quick strikes over the plate. Then there were three balls. The next pitch looked good to Phil. He ignored his manager's orders and swung savagely at the ball.

He didn't quite get all of his bat on the pitch. He fouled it, and the ball flew back, over the head of the Coney Island catcher and under the mask of the home plate umpire, hitting him on his Adam's apple.

The umpire was as mad as a hornet and, as soon as he regained his wind, called Phil every name in the book.

When finally he yelled "play ball," Phil just froze at the plate. He wasn't going to swing at anything again, not in that game, anyway.

The pitch, luckily for Phil, was so wide that the umpire couldn't call him out on strikes.

"Ball four!" whispered the umpire, hoarsely, and for the fifth time in the game Phil walked.

The Ridgewood Robins finally did win the game and the sandlot championship of Brooklyn, and Mr. Willenbucher was so happy that he didn't even think about bawling out his four-foot star for his disobedience.

3

The Education
of a Star

After his graduation from Public School 68, Phil went on to Richmond Hill High. The high school was a considerable distance from home, and, like most freshmen, Phil found himself among a sea of strangers. He was naturally shy, and here, no longer among friends, he became more conscious of his size.

Still, Phil reported for the first call for baseball practice. But when his best friend, Johnny Zimmerlich, was dropped because of his poor grades, Phil quit the team. He just didn't feel he could play without Johnny.

That first year at Richmond Hill was tough for Phil. It wasn't easy getting used to his new surroundings. And it bothered him even more not to play baseball for the school.

Sophomore year was better. Johnny Zimmerlich picked up on his studies and was again eligible for the baseball squad. With a friend at his side, Phil didn't hesitate to answer coach Al Kunitz's call for candidates.

Al Kunitz had played ball when he was at Columbia University. Although he had weighed a mere 135 pounds, he was one of the best catchers who had ever put on a uniform for the Columbia Lions. He knew his baseball. He also knew talent when he saw it. Al Kunitz, perhaps more than anyone else, would be responsible for Phil Rizzuto's brilliant career on the diamond.

"I play the outfield," said Phil, responding to the coach's query about his preferred position.

"OK," said Kunitz. "Let's see what you can do."

Phil, no more than five feet tall at the time, trotted out onto the field. Kunitz followed his play carefully. He scrutinized the way every candidate for the baseball squad played, carefully, critically, knowingly.

He shook his head when Phil was done with his workout.

"You're too small for the outfield," he said.

Phil protested and told him how he had played the outfield for the Ridgewood Robins.

"That's fine," responded Kunitz. "You can play ball all right, but not the outfield. With a pair of hands like yours, and that strong arm, you'll make a great infielder. A *great* infielder!"

To strengthen his argument the coach spoke of that all-time great, Rabbit Marranville, who stood just five-foot, five-inches tall.

"He was a midget," said Kunitz, "but he became a star!"

Actually, it didn't matter to Phil where he played, just so long as he played. As for Al Kunitz, he recognized the potential in little Phil Rizzuto and gave him a great deal of individual coaching.

He taught Phil how to bunt.

"A ballplayer has to hit the ball on the nose three times in a game to get one good base hit, on the average. A well-placed bunt will make up for all those well-hit balls that land right in the glove of an outfielder."

Phil would hit the ball a long way once in a while, but he was never a power hitter. Bunting was an art he learned quickly, and it would help his batting average throughout his career.

Al Kunitz also taught Phil the technique of the hit-and-run play.

"The man on first will break for second as the pitcher winds up. The second baseman or sometimes the shortstop will head for that base to make the putout in case of an attempted steal. That gives the batter more space to hit between first and second, or second and third, depending on who goes for second. Got it?" Young Phil Rizzuto got it. He worked on it. He would become one of the best hit-and-run men in baseball.

Al Kunitz was a fine teacher, a great coach. He taught his players everything there was to know about baseball, and a number of them played professional ball, some in the major leagues. Second baseman Ralph Benzenberg was signed by a New York Giants farm club. Marius Russo wound up on the pitching staff of the New York Yankees from 1939–46. But Phil Rizzuto would become the greatest star he had taught, groomed, and coached.

Phil played third base for Richmond Hill High, and he was every bit as good as his coach had expected, perhaps better. In his second year with the team, Phil was the leading hitter. He hit for an average of .354 and was elected captain of the club. He got an All-Scholastic rating. The *Long Island Press*, a highly respected daily, named him New York City's best high school third baseman. Al Kunitz was now sure that Phil, despite his size, could play major league baseball. And as a good teacher, and friend, the coach decided that he was going to get his star pupil every opportunity to prove it.

"You're going places," said the coach to Phil, "but we've

got a lot of work ahead of us. I want you to get out there and play all the baseball you can. I want you to eat and drink and think baseball. I want you to live the game, every day."

"I play with the Glendale Browns every Saturday and Sunday," answered Phil enthusiastically.

The Glendale Browns was a neighborhood team playing in a league known as the Queens Alliance. It was an amateur league, with players ranging in age from sixteen to twenty-one. The money for their uniforms and other equipment was raised by donations and projects such as selling raffle tickets.

"That's fine," said Al Kunitz, "but it's not enough. What are you going to do during vacation?"

"I don't know," said Phil.

"Find yourself a team," ordered the coach. "Play ball."

And Phil followed orders.

That summer, 1934, not quite sixteen years old, Rizzuto played semipro ball for Floral Park in Nassau County, Long Island. It was the first time he earned money playing ball. It wasn't much. There was no fixed salary. At the end of the season, after paying off expenses, the team divided the profits. Phil collected the princely sum of $120. He had played shortstop in eighty games under the unlikely name of Reilly. He had to take on an assumed name if he was going to continue playing amateur baseball at Richmond Hill High.

Phil had played shortstop well at Floral Park, and it was at shortstop that he would play for Richmond Hill in his last year on the team. Coach Al Kunitz was more excited than ever about his young star's prospects.

He got the St. Louis Cardinals organization to send a scout to watch a game Richmond Hill played against another high school, John Adams. Phil made three solid hits in that game.

He fielded his position flawlessly. At one point in the game, he made a great diving stop of a ball that had "hit" written all over it and, from a sitting position, threw his man out. Phil had a strong arm and whipped the ball to first. He knew there was a Cardinal scout watching him, and he felt sure he was making a good impression. With an uncharacteristic touch of confidence, Phil fully expected the scout to offer him a contract right then and there on the ballfield.

He was going to be disappointed.

"Pretty good," said the scout to the young fellow, "but I don't want to kid you. You're just not big enough for a ballplayer. You're too small, kid. I'm sorry."

Phil was crestfallen. He'd had his hopes up too high, much too high.

And what was that business about his height? Coach Kunitz had said that Rabbit Marranville had been a midget, but still a great baseball player. Didn't anybody else know that?

"Don't you worry, Phil," said Kunitz. "The man's blind. There'll be other scouts, and we'll get you there."

Al Kunitz meant what he said. No one was going to stop him from getting Phil Rizzuto into professional ball.

He got a Boston Red Sox scout to look over Rizzuto. The scout, named Egan, carefully watched Phil, and he was impressed. He was impressed enough to offer Rizzuto $250 to sign with a Red Sox farm club.

"Didn't I tell you!" exclaimed the jubilant Kunitz.

"Yeah!" said Phil exuberantly. "But let me talk it over with my mother and father."

Egan and Phil shook hands on it and agreed to meet the next morning.

Two hundred and fifty dollars was a lot of money in those

days, and his parents were delighted with the news Phil brought home. As for Phil, dreams of baseball glory filled the dark hours that night.

He was up bright and early, and was early enough at the spot where he was to meet Egan. But Egan wasn't there. Phil waited impatiently. Still no Egan. He began to worry that perhaps he had gotten the date and place mixed up. No Egan. He must have waited two hours, and the Red Sox scout still didn't show up.

"Maybe he forgot," said Phil. "Maybe he didn't think I was good enough."

But Al Kunitz was far from giving up on his young protégé. He started to think that the way for Phil to break into the ranks of professional baseball was to play in college. Today many professional ballplayers come out of college. Back in 1935, there weren't too many baseball men with college degrees, but Eddie Collins, Christy Mathewson, Lou Gehrig, and Frankie Frisch, all great ballplayers, had come to the game from seats of higher learning.

George Vecsey of the *Long Island Press*, and later the *New York Times*, was at a game Richmond Hill played at Columbia's Baker Field against the Columbia Lions' freshman squad. Ralph Benzenberg, the Richmond Hill second baseman, starred in that game, and Vecsey suggested to the Lions' coach, Ralph Furey, that Benzenberg might be a good player for the Columbia baseball team.

"I'd rather take the little runt," said Furey, speaking of Phil. "He's got all the makings of a good player. He can hit, he's fast, and he's got what it takes to make a fine shortstop."

That's what Al Kunitz thought, too, but Phil didn't have the grades required for admission to Columbia.

He came closer to getting into Fordham. Jack Coffey, head
of athletics and baseball coach of the university, had him up at
the school for a workout and liked what he saw. He thought,
too, that Phil might be of some help to the Ram football team,
coached by the great Jim Crowley. He figured Phil, with his
great speed, would make a fine scatback.

Phil wanted a little time to think over this two-sport offer,
but by the time he decided to take it, Jack Coffey was away in
Europe for the summer, and no one Phil contacted at the
Fordham athletic office had ever heard of him, let alone the
deal that Coffey had offered.

Phil was back in school in the spring of 1936, but he was
having a difficult time with French and other courses, and he
was playing hookey too often to keep up with his classwork.
So, Phil quit school. It was just too much for him. Later on,
when he made good as a ballplayer, Phil often would say he
was sorry that he did not graduate. In 1948 the school held its
seventy-fifth anniversary celebration, and students who had become successful were awarded diplomas, so Phil became a
certified graduate.

Phil got a job assisting a man lift barrels of syrup and 100-
pound bags of sugar for the S. Gumpert Co., a manufacturer
of food stuffs. He could handle the heavy lifting because he
had always worked hard to develop his shoulders and arms,
and now they were strong and muscular. He also played ball
for the company in the old Brooklyn Industrial League, on the
Prospect Park Parade Grounds.

Meanwhile, Al Kunitz kept trying to put Phil in touch with
major league clubs. He had arranged for those dismal tryouts
with the Dodgers and the Giants the year before. Now he went
after the New York Yankees.

Paul Krichell was the leading Yankee scout. In 1911 and 1912 Krichell had been a catcher for the St. Louis Browns, and he had been working for the Yankee organization for many years, keeping the Yankees well supplied with talent. Krich, prodded by Kunitz, had seen Phil play and realized that the youngster, despite his size, rated at least a tryout, so Phil was invited to a tryout at Yankee Stadium, late in August.

This time there were only twenty-five young hopefuls on the field. Phil was confident that his talent really would be noticed in such a small group of players.

The players were divided into two teams, and, for three mornings, before the Yankees took the field for their pregame warmups, the kids played a regular five-inning game, carefully watched and supervised by Krichell and manager Joe McCarthy's number one coach, Art Fletcher.

"That's Lou Gehrig!"

"There goes Bill Dickey!"

Phil Rizzuto just stood there in awe, watching the big men swing their bats and run out onto the field.

There was Red Ruffing, Lefty Gomez, Frank Crosetti, Tony Lazzeri.

"Hyah, kid," said Tony Lazzeri, and the youngster from Glendale could hardly open his mouth to return the Yankee great's greeting.

"I was talking to Tony Lazzeri!" he boasted, a big grin on his face, to anyone who would listen. "He said, 'Hyah' and I said, 'Hyah.' "

It was wonderful!

As the tryouts came to a close, Paul Krichell turned to Art Fletcher. "What do you think?" he asked the coach.

There were a number of good prospects among those kids.

There was Tommy Holmes, who would star for the Boston Braves in the 1940s, and there was Jim Prendergast, who would pitch briefly for the Braves in 1948.

"I'll take the little one out there at short," said Fletcher, at one time himself a fine shortstop for the New York Giants. "I like his speed, his reflexes. He's got lightning in his hands. He's got a good arm. And he can hit the ball, too."

Joe McCarthy had been watching the kids this last day of the tryouts, too.

"Yeah," the manager said. "That little fellow is the best I've seen all day, but he's too short to play in Yankee Stadium."

"He's big enough," retorted Krichell confidently.

It was Art Fletcher who approached the little guy at the end of the morning.

"We think we can use you, kid," he said. "Would you like to play with one of our farm clubs?"

"Would I?" Young Phil's feet weren't touching the ground. "Yes, sir! Yes, sir!"

"OK. You're on," said Fletcher. "You'll be getting a call from us in a couple of days, and we'll have a contract for you."

Phil couldn't get into his street clothes and to a telephone booth fast enough.

"Mama! I made it! I made it, Mama!"

The next call was to Al Kunitz.

"I made it, Al! I made it!"

Phil sat at home, glued to the telephone, waiting for that call from the New York Yankees' front office.

The call would come, but first there was a call from an unexpected source, the Boston Red Sox. Evidently there had been a Red Sox scout that day at Yankee Stadium, and he had been impressed by the youngster.

"We'd like to sign you up with us," said the Boston scout, "but I've got to check on somebody in Kentucky first. You can expect a contract from us in a couple of days."

The somebody he had to check on in Kentucky was Harold (Peewee) Reese. Reese would be signed by the Red Sox and wind up as one of the greatest shortstops in baseball history, playing for the Brooklyn Dodgers. When Boston finally got around to mailing Phil Rizzuto a contract, it was too late. Paul Krichell had called with an offer, and Phil became a member of the Yankees' organization.

There were some minor details to be settled before Phil signed the contract, but Mrs. Rizzuto would take care of those details in time. All that mattered to young Phil Rizzuto, that bright day in August of 1936, was that at last he was going to play professional baseball.

4

Onward and Upward

Paul Krichell spread out the contract before Phil and his parents.

"We'll be sending you down to Butler," said Paul.

"Where is that?" asked Mrs. Rizzuto.

"Pennsylvania," said Paul. "It's not very far from New York," added Krichell, anticipating the next question. "Butler is our farm club in the Pennsylvania State League," he put in for Phil's information.

"That's all right with me," said Phil.

"You'll get seventy-five dollars a month, for the duration of the season," said Paul.

Seventy-five dollars a month sounded like big money to Phil. It was a lot more than most kids his age were earning in those early years after the Depression. But the Yanks had a farm club in Virginia, and the season in Virginia was a month longer than the season in Pennsylvania. That would mean an extra seventy-five dollars for Phil. He asked Paul Krichell about it.

"Sure," said Paul. "We've got a club in Bassett. You can go there, if you like."

It didn't matter to Krichell. Bassett and Butler were both Class D clubs. It mattered to young Rizzuto.

"I'll take Bassett then," said Phil.

"OK," said Paul, and, giving Mama his pen, he said, "You'll have to sign this, Mrs. Rizzuto. Phil's still too young."

Phil was too young, legally, to sign the contract, but before Mrs. Rizzuto would sign the document, she had a couple of questions she wanted answered.

"Mr. Krichell," she said, "Phil has never been away from home."

"There are many boys down there who have never been away from home," said Paul.

"Yes, Mr. Krichell, but where is Phil going to live, where is he going to eat, who is going to take care of his laundry? Suppose he gets sick?"

"Don't you worry any, Mrs. Rizzuto. We'll find him a nice family to live with, a nice clean place, and good food to eat. He won't get sick, and, if he needs a doctor, we'll have one right there."

"Are you sure?" asked Phil's mother with concern.

"Sure, Mrs. Rizzuto. Your son is going to live a good and healthy life in Bassett. Believe me, Mrs. Rizzuto. Believe me."

Mrs. Rizzuto was still hesitant.

"Sign it, Mama," urged an anxious Phil. "Everything is going to be all right. Please, sign it!"

Still reluctant, she finally signed the contract. After all, she was sending her boy away from home, and, for her, Virginia was *very* far away from home.

But Phil was jubilant. Seventy-five dollars a month to play professional baseball! It was as much as he had ever dreamed of.

There was no bonus for Phil on signing. Such an idea never even occurred to him. In fact, the practice of paying a player a bonus on signing was still a long way off.

Years later, Ed Barrow, a former general manager of the New York Yankees, would say, "Rizzuto cost me fifteen cents: ten for postage and five for the cup of coffee we gave him the last day he worked out at the Stadium."

The Yankees certainly could not have made a better deal, considering that one day Rizzuto would be ranked as one of baseball's greatest shortstops.

Phil arrived in Bassett in the spring of 1937 with ten dollars in his pocket, or rather ten dollars pinned to his undershirt. His father had pinned it there to make sure that the money wasn't lost or stolen in transit. Phil got off the train, watched it pull out of the station, then stared across the tracks at a drugstore, a movie house, a ramshackle structure that passed for a hotel, and a diner. That's all there was to Bassett, Virginia.

Suddenly, Phil had a hollow feeling in the pit of his stomach, and an awful loneliness overcame him. Here he was, a long way from home, a long way from everybody and everything he knew. It was as if he had been abruptly dropped down in the middle of a desert and he was lost.

It was unearthly quiet. Where was the hustle and bustle he had lived with all his life, the talk, the shoving of crowds, the screeching of wheels, the tooting of horns that had assailed his eyes and ears? Bassett certainly wasn't Brooklyn.

Where is everybody? Where is everything? he wanted to yell.

If there had been a train headed back for New York, he might very well have hopped on it. Fortunately for Phil, and for baseball, there was no such train, not that day, anyway. And fortunately, too, there were a couple of familiar faces, when Phil finally caught up with the Bassett ballclub.

There was Herb Karpel, who had been a pal of his at Richmond Hill High School. More important for Phil, there was Ray White, the manager of the Bassett club. White had managed a semipro team for which Phil had played in Brooklyn. White knew Phil's potential, and it was this knowledge that kept Phil playing baseball. Young Rizzuto wasn't the only one trying to make shortstop on the Bassett nine, and a couple of the others were perhaps more polished than the kid from Brooklyn. But Ray White had always liked what Rizzuto had showed him, and he liked it even more in Bassett. Bassett, according to its league rules, could carry only one shortstop on its roster. White selected Phil.

It was these same league rules that made for the most traumatic experience in young Rizzuto's life.

Class D clubs were limited to a roster of fifteen men. Bassett had six pitchers, two catchers, and seven others to cover the other seven positions on the diamond. If Ray White needed a pinch hitter, he had to send a pitcher to the plate. If a player in the field got hurt or was sick, a pitcher had to fill in for him. A Class D player had to be really hurt or sick before White replaced him with one of his six pitchers. That's why Phil kept playing shortstop for Bassett long after he had any right to be on the field, in a situation that nearly cost him his baseball career.

Phil had gotten off to a great start that first season in pro ball. His fielding was brilliant and he was hitting the ball with authority. Bassett was riding high, in first place in the Virginia League. The fans were flocking to the ballpark, Phil had become the most popular player Bassett had ever had, and Ray White was sending enthusiastic reports to the front office in New York on the progress of his club, and particularly on the performance of his young shortstop.

A month into the season, however, Phil developed a sore muscle, a charley horse. It was painful and it hampered his performance in the field, but he kept playing.

Ray White would knead the muscle, massage it, pound it, before the game and after. Ray was not only Bassett's manager, but also its bus driver, secretary, trainer, and everything else.

"How does it feel, kid?"

"Better."

But it wasn't better. It was worse. It became more difficult for him to go after a ball, field it, throw it. He just couldn't pivot at second base to make the double play.

"Maybe you ought to rest it for a couple of days," said Ray White.

"And who'll play short?" asked Phil.

There was nobody to play short.

"I'll play," said Phil, and he hobbled out onto the field.

But that leg wasn't going to get better by itself, and it got so swollen that even an umpire noticed.

"You'd better get that leg looked at, kid," said the man in blue. "I've never seen a leg look that bad before."

It got so bad that young Rizzuto just couldn't take it anymore.

"Maybe I ought to see a doctor," he finally said to White.

White agreed and drove Phil to Roanoke. That was the nearest town with a hospital. The doctor took one look at the leg and said, "We'll have to operate."

"Operate!?" yelled Phil.

He'd never been to a hospital before, let alone on an operating table.

"It can't be that bad," he said.

He was scared. He was scared to death when he heard the rest of what the doctor had to say.

"Looks like you've got gangrene in that leg," explained the doctor. "You wait much longer and I'm afraid we'll have to cut it off."

Phil turned to Ray White for support.

But Ray just shook his head. "You've got no choice," he said.

"You *do* have a choice," the doctor corrected. "The operation or the leg."

"When?" asked Phil.

"Right now," said the doctor. "How old are you?"

"Eighteen," he answered.

"We'll need parental permission for the operation," the doctor went on.

"My parents are in Brooklyn," protested Phil.

"We can't wait," said the doctor. "We'll operate now and get permission later."

That's how critical the situation was.

They did call Mrs. Rizzuto, but Phil was rolled into surgery at once. They had to cut away muscle that had already been eaten away by gangrene and attach one end of the good muscle to the other end of good muscle. It took thirty-seven stitches to sew him up, from his knee to his groin. Phil still carries the scar, but his leg was all right, and, after two and a half months of convalescence, he was back in uniform and as good as ever. Phil owed much to that umpire, Ray White, and especially to the surgeon in Roanoke.

Rizzuto played sixty-seven games for Bassett in his first year as a pro. His fielding, as Paul Krichell had expected, was of major league caliber. His hitting was outstanding and surprised everyone. In sixty-seven games he collected eighty-eight hits for a .310 average. Seventeen of his hits had been doubles, five triples, and five home runs. The little guy had learned from Al Kunitz and had worked hard. He knew how to bunt for a base hit, how to work the hit and run play, and once in a while he could hit the ball with real power. Phil played well enough in that first year as a pro to spark his club to the Bi-State pennant. He was delivering on his potential, and in a big way.

In 1938, Ray White received recognition for his work from the Yankee front office. He was promoted and went to manage the Norfolk, Virginia, team in the Class B Piedmont League. And he asked George Weiss, who at that time was farm director of the Yankees, to send Rizzuto up with him. Of course he had no difficulty convincing Weiss, and it was a nice move for Phil, but it didn't come easily.

Norfolk already had a good shortstop, Claude Corbitt. Corbitt had been a star ballplayer at nearby Duke University. He was a southerner. He was a good hitter and a great favorite with the Norfolk fans. They didn't care too much for having a northerner, Ray White, manage the club. They liked even less the idea of a northerner, Phil Rizzuto, displacing their local boy, Corbitt, at short.

For the first time in his life, Phil Rizzuto heard boos directed at him from the stands. Ray White, of course, got his share of booing, too. The local sportswriters filled their columns with scurrilous attacks on the two northerners. The radio broadcasters contributed to the barrage of criticism. The Norfolk fans threatened to boycott the team. Things got so bad that Ray White had to contact George Weiss to ask for advice on the situation. George came up with a solution, and it was a good one. Corbitt was promoted to Augusta in the Class A League. Rizzuto stayed behind with Ray White and Norfolk. No one—ballplayer, manager, fans, the media— could complain about that.

Corbitt ended up kicking around in the minors and then playing a total of 215 games in four seasons in the majors. He never made it big, which is the case with many young minor leaguers who look promising.

Phil rewarded Ray White for his confidence in him. It didn't take him long to win over the Norfolk fans, not the way he played ball. Eventually, he became the most popular player Norfolk ever had, and for good reason. Phil batted .336 that year and was voted to the all-star team by the sportswriters. The little guy was headed for even better years, and fast, but not at Norfolk.

In 1939, Phil was promoted to Kansas City in the American Association, the top league in the minors. It was from the American Association that a man jumped up to the big leagues, if he was major league material.

Phil was joined at Kansas City by his second-base pal at Norfolk, Jerry Priddy. Priddy had come up in baseball through Los Angeles, Arkansas, and Missouri, and then he went to Norfolk. He and Rizzuto became the classiest infielders in the minors, developing a double-play combination that soon had everybody taking notice. They were a great defensive duo, with sure hands and strong arms. They were also inseparable pals, on the playing field and off, as inseparable as Mutt and Jeff of comic strip fame, and about as different, too.

Jerry Priddy stood six feet tall and weighed 180 pounds.

Phil had grown to five feet, five inches and, after a hearty dinner, weighed 154 pounds. The big guy was rough and tough, an aggressive player, and he appointed himself Phil's guardian and champion. Anybody who gave Phil any trouble on the field or off had to contend with Jerry and, more than likely, would end up in a fight with the big guy. The only time Priddy wouldn't step in to protect Phil was when a teammate played a trick on his buddy.

There was the time, for instance, during spring training down South, when some of the players took Phil snipe hunting. A snipe is a long-billed wading bird. The "hunt" took them deep into an orange grove, about six miles out of camp.

"Here, hold this flashlight," one of his teammates told Phil. "You're going to catch the snipe."

"How?" asked Phil.

"Easy," he said. "Here's a bag and a loaf of bread."

"What do I do with 'em?"

"We'll tell you. Just listen. You stand here while we hide. Then we'll come running out, yelling and scaring the snipe."

"How about me? Won't I be scared?"

"Naw. The snipe'll be running right at you. Just flash the light in the bag and throw in a piece of bread. The snipe'll run right into the bag. Got it?"

Phil wasn't too sure but he said, "Yeah, got it," and everyone left him alone in the dark, except for his flashlight, in the orange grove.

After only a few minutes, which seemed like hours to Phil, who was feeling more and more nervous, all the guys came out of hiding, running and yelling loud enough to scare the oranges off the trees.

Phil followed orders. He flashed the light, threw some

bread into the bag, then flashed the light again and threw in more bread.

"Where's the snipe? Where's the snipe?" yelled Rizzuto. His teammates just broke up and began to howl.

"No snipe?" said Phil, finally catching on to the trick.

But it was all in fun. There was no malice. Everybody loved Phil Rizzuto. He was easy to kid. He was perhaps the most gullible fellow who ever played ball.

The very next spring training they pulled that snipe trick on Rizzuto again. This time Phil was supposed to be a leader, and a rookie the victim. However, when they were deep in the orange grove, everyone, including the rookie, disappeared, and Phil was left all alone, but not for long. This time his teammates had gotten the town sheriff in on the act, and he was on the scene in a jiffy.

"What are you doing here?" the sheriff asked Phil.

"Nothing," he answered, too scared to say anything else.

"Prowling!" barked the sheriff, putting on a good act. "We don't like prowlers around here!"

Then he clapped a pair of handcuffs on Phil and took him off to the town jail.

Poor Phil spent a couple of hours sitting in that jail cell, not knowing what to do, wondering how many years they'd send him up for, worrying about what his mother and father would think, and about what would happen to his baseball career. Finally, after what seemed like an eternity, all his "friends" showed up, and, along with the sheriff, they had a mighty good laugh at Phil's expense.

It would have been understandable if Phil had gone into a fit of rage. But he didn't. Phil just wasn't made that way. He rarely got angry. He never lost his temper. He was always an easygoing fellow, the easiest to get along with. Besides, he knew there was never any malice in the tricks his friends played on him, and they would constantly play tricks on him. One night he found frogs in his bed. Another time just before a game he discovered his spikes had been nailed to the floor. His letters were ripped up so he couldn't read them; his underwear torn. And that wasn't all. But Phil took it, took it well, and laughed with the rest of the players when the trick was discovered.

There were no tricks on the diamond, however. There, in Kansas City, playing for manager Billy Meyer, who would later manage the Pittsburgh Pirates, it was all business, and Priddy and Rizzuto shone like a twin diamond stickpin, as they sparked the Kansas City club to successive pennants in 1939 and 1940. They were the most talked-about pair in baseball. Ed Barrow, president and general manager of the Yankees at that time, was offered a quarter of a million dollars for the keystone duo. In current currency that would come to several million dollars. He was offered $150,000 for Rizzuto alone.

Everybody who was knowledgeable in baseball was particularly impressed with Rizzuto. His hitting was considerably better than average for a shortstop, and his fielding was just super. He scooped up everything hit between second and third, and no one had ever ranged to his left as well as Phil. Often, when Jerry Priddy had been pulled out of position at second, Phil would scoot across the bag, pick up the ball in the hole, and throw his man out at first. "Scooter"—that's what his teammate, third-baseman Billy Hitchcock, called him at Kansas City. He would yell after a good play, "Phil, you're not running after the ball, you're *scooting*." The nickname stuck.

Both Priddy and Phil were ready for the big leagues in 1940 and could very well have been called up by the Yankees. But, under the fabulous Joe McCarthy, the Yanks had won their fourth straight pennant and fourth straight World Series in 1939, and they had no shortage of talent. The Yankees had the best second baseman in the majors, Joe Gordon, and Frank Crosetti was an ace shortstop. McCarthy wasn't about to make a change in his winning lineup. Phil and Jerry had to bide their time in Kansas City for another year, and it did neither team nor ballplayers any harm.

Priddy hit .306 and drove in 112 runs for KC in 1940. Phil, just twenty-one years old, did even better, amazing all by lashing 201 hits, including ten homers and ten triples, for a sensational .347 average. And he led the American Association in stolen bases with thirty-five.

In 1940, the fans voted Rizzuto the most popular Kansas City player, and the *Sporting News* named him the Minor League Player of the Year.

After such a great year, it was no wonder that sportswriters and others were predicting that Phil Rizzuto would prove as great a sensation at Yankee Stadium as Joltin' Joe DiMaggio.

5

The Rookie

Phil's contract as a rookie with the Yankees gave him $5,000 a year, if he made the team. Ed Barrow was a tough negotiator and didn't pay any fancy salaries in 1941. But he needn't have worried about a salary hassle with the youngster; Phil wasn't thinking of numbers, he was dreaming of pinstripes, a Yankee uniform. Nobody had dreamed more of becoming a major league ballplayer than had the kid from Brooklyn. He was an excited kid, indeed, leaving home in 1941 for the Yankees' spring training camp in St. Petersburg, Florida.

He was nervous, too, and a bit scared. After all, he'd played only four years in the minors and he had heard lots of stories of players who had been great in the minor leagues and come a cropper in the majors.

He wasn't particularly encouraged, either, when he got his first look at Miller Huggins Field in St. Petersburg, the park named for the once-great, diminutive (5'6½") manager of the New York club. Miller Huggins Field wasn't an imposing edifice. It wasn't even as big as some of the parks he had played in in the minors. The seats were painted a pale green, and the whole atmosphere was uninviting. What was worse, he couldn't even get into the clubhouse.

42

"Outside, you!"

It was Fred Logan. Logan had been the Yankees' club-house man for years.

"I'm Phil Rizzuto," the youngster said.

"So what?" countered Logan. "No kids allowed in here. Now, beat it!"

Little Phil may have never made it into the clubhouse that day if Lefty Gomez, the great Yankee pitcher, hadn't sauntered over, a towel wrapped around his middle and a big friendly grin on his face.

"Come on, Fred," he said to the clubhouse man. "Don't you know who this cockroach is?"

Logan shook his head. How would he know Phil Rizzuto?

"Come on, Phil," said Lefty, grabbing Phil by his arm. "Get in here before the ducks start stepping all over you."

There were ducks in the yard in front of the Yankee club-house, lots of ducks. Phil had grown to five feet five inches now, but to Lefty Gomez he was just a shrimp.

Phil let Lefty's gibe go. He knew he was in for a lot of ribbing about his size, but he was used to it by now. However, when he found his locker in the clubhouse sandwiched between Bill Dickey's and Red Ruffing's, two big men, he was all but ready to turn and run. They were not only big in size, they were giants in the baseball world.

It wasn't going to be easy for the young fellow. It never is for anyone moving into close company for the first time, and the Yankees were close company. Besides, the vets had their loyalties, and none of them cared to see such stalwarts as Gordon and Crosetti challenged for positions in the Yankee lineup.

Joe McCarthy, however, was the most difficult man for Phil to understand in his first weeks of spring training.

"He didn't seem to be looking at anybody in particular," recalled Phil, "but I couldn't help feeling he was taking in everything I did."

That was McCarthy, all right. Sitting or standing behind the first base line, nothing escaped his attention.

"Can you do the buck-and-wing dance?" he once asked Phil in the spring camp.

Phil looked at the skipper. *Is he for real?* he asked himself.

"Sure, I can buck-and-wing," said Phil, a sheepish grin on his face.

"I don't mean when you're dancing out there with some band playing," said Joe. "Can you buck-and-wing on the field?"

He showed Phil what he meant, taking little mincing steps at shortstop.

"That's the way you go after ground balls. It'll help you get into position for the ball, help your throw to first base. Practice it."

Phil practiced it. He was beginning to get an education on how to play his position in the big leagues.

"You jam your spikes into the ground when you go deep for a ball," instructed Joe McCarthy, still in spring training. "Let your right foot slide to a stop. That way you're better balanced to make the play and throw."

McCarthy had Joe Gordon demonstrate the technique and Phil nodded in understanding.

"Show him again, Joe," said McCarthy. Gordon demonstrated, and Phil worked at it until he was sliding that right foot automatically.

Coaches Fletcher and Schulte had him on the field going after balls hit between the shortstop hole and third base. They had him work on his throwing, insisting that he change his throw from sidearm to overhand. When he rushed his throws, eager to get the batter at first base, he began to lose his accuracy, and his confidence. That's when Joe Gordon and Frank Crosetti came into the picture.

"Don't rush your throw. You lose the grip on the ball. Take your time. Unless he catches you flatfooted, you'll have more than enough time to catch the fastest of runners."

It didn't take long for the youngster to regain his accuracy, and his confidence as well.

Phil was scheduled to take over Frank Crosetti's spot at shortstop. Crosetti had been a magnificent shortstop for nine years but showed signs of slowing down. Yet Crosetti was a remarkable man and held no grudge against Phil. Perhaps more than anyone else, he worked closely with Phil, and he taught him the little tricks he had picked up through his many years with the Yankees. Crosetti was helping Phil to take his job away. That was the Yankee spirit, and Frank was a Yankee all the way.

"You want to play in a few feet," Frank would say to the kid. "Go more to your left."

He taught Phil how to slide into a base.

"When you get to first base," advised Crosetti, "pick up a handful of dirt in each fist and hold it there. When you slide into second, you'll hold your hands naturally up in the air. The way you're sliding now, you'll break a finger."

After four great winning years, the Yankees had dropped to third place in 1940 as the Detroit Tigers won the pennant by the scant margin of one game over Cleveland. The Yankees had finished one game behind the scrappy Indians.

Joe McCarthy had to make some changes in the lineup. He intended to insert Priddy at second base and Rizzuto at short.

Crosetti had had a poor year in 1940, Dickey's hitting had dropped off from a strong .302 in 1939 to .247, and Lefty Gomez had only managed three wins. The skipper felt he couldn't keep hard-hitting Joe Gordon out of the lineup and so tried him at first base. He had Red Rolfe at third and in the outfield the great trio of Joe DiMaggio, Charlie Keller, and Tommy Henrich. The stars of the pitching staff were Red Ruffing and Spud Chandler.

But Gordon looked strange and felt stranger at first base. The rookies Rizzuto and Priddy were understandably nervous in their first couple of games in the big leagues. The Yankees had lost the 1940 championship because of a ragged start, and Joe McCarthy wasn't going to let another slow start rob him of the pennant in 1941. After the Yankees lost a few close games, he acted quickly.

Phil was sitting with Priddy in the dugout before a game, when suddenly Priddy was ordered into the manager's office in the clubhouse.

Jerry shrugged his shoulders. What did McCarthy want of him? He wanted to ask but didn't dare.

Jerry wasn't gone very long. He came back to the dugout and sat down on the bench next to Phil. He was fighting back tears.

"I'm not playing today," he said.

"Sorry," Phil began, but he didn't have time to say more than that. Art Fletcher told him that Joe McCarthy wanted to see him, too.

Phil's heart sank. He knew what was coming.

"Sit down, Phil," said McCarthy, when he entered the manager's office. "I'm going to give you a little rest."

Phil was shocked. It was the first time he had ever been

benched. Worse, he was sure that he hadn't made the grade and that McCarthy was letting him down easy.

"I'm just beginning to get the hang of things, Mr. McCarthy. Why don't you let me stay in there?" pleaded young Phil.

McCarthy shook his head.

"You'll get another view of the game from the bench, Phil," he said. "You'll sit near me. There are situations in the game I'll explain to you. You just listen and remember what I tell you. It's going to help your game a lot."

McCarthy put rookie Johnny Sturm at first base, Joe Gordon back at second, and Frank Crosetti at short, and the Yankees began to click. Phil sat next to McCarthy on the bench and watched and listened.

Joe Gordon advised, "You've been trying too hard, pressing."

Crosetti told him, "You've been too tight. You've been throwing the ball before you've had it."

"You're so anxious up at bat," said Crosetti, "that you've been swinging at balls nowhere near the plate."

On one occasion he watched Joe Gordon run a relay ball into the infield and stop the man on first from going to third on a hit.

"You don't always throw the ball," said Joe McCarthy to his rookie. "If Joe threw that ball to third, the runner might have made it. You don't give up an extra base when you don't have to. Sometimes the best thing to do is hold up on a throw."

In one game Tommy Henrich was up at bat with a runner at third. He took a low pitch for a strike.

"Why doesn't he bunt the run in?" asked Phil, impatiently.

"Don't second guess," said his skipper.

"Make him pitch to you!" yelled Phil to a hitter, another time, when the opposing hurler was wild.

"Why?" asked Joe McCarthy, quietly. "He's having a tough time getting it over the plate. He's got to ease up to get it in. It's a perfect spot to hit on the first pitch. It'll probably be a cripple he's trying to sneak across the plate."

For almost a month, Phil sat on the bench, his eyes wide, studying the game, soaking up all the wisdom he could from one of the greatest managers in the history of baseball. When Frank Crosetti was spiked and taken out of the game, the Scooter was ready.

"Get in there, kid," said McCarthy, and this time Scooter went in to play for a long, long time.

Joe DiMaggio, Bill Dickey, Charlie Keller, Tommy Henrich, and Joe Gordon were hammering the ball, driving opposing pitchers out of the box with regularity. The club was hitting at a .300 clip. The Yanks were at the top of the league and running away from the pack. The New York club had regained its confidence and was headed once more for the pennant and a World Series.

With that kind of atmosphere in the clubhouse and on the diamond, the pressure on the rookie Rizzuto was off. He played up to his potential in the field and, with Joe Gordon at second, the Yanks had an outstanding combination up the middle. They were so good that even the players on the opposing teams would stop to watch the brilliant duo go through their routines in the pregame workout.

That month on the bench, with Joe McCarthy at his side, had worked wonders for the Scooter. Even McCarthy was surprised by the change in the play of his rookie, the sharpness, the keenness, the enthusiasm—and it was his enthusiasm that was infectious. If the club hadn't paid much attention to the rookie down at spring training and into the first weeks of the '41 season, they were all well aware of him now, and they couldn't help loving him for both his enthusiasm and his obvious boyish naiveté. He invited kidding and all those tricks they played on him, though not when Joe McCarthy was skipper— Joe was too serious a man for that kind of tomfoolery.

The fans grew to love the Scooter quickly, too, and he proved to be the sensation they had expected. No, he wasn't a slugger like Joe DiMaggio, but he had other attributes. In his first season with the Yankees, both in the field and at bat, he was outstanding. He was the team's second best hitter, next to DiMaggio, compiling a .307 average in 133 games, with twenty doubles, nine triples, and three home runs. He scored sixty-five times, batted in forty-six runs, and stole fourteen bases. Phil was good enough in his first season as a Yankee to win accolades as the Yankees' number one rookie of the year.

And, on the verge of playing in the World Series, nobody was more excited than Phil. A World Series, and in his first year! It was a dream come true.

The Yankees were World Series veterans. They had won sixteen games and lost only three in the four World Series from 1936 through 1939. It was a relatively calm bunch of ballplayers who approached the world championship games. Not so their opponents, the Brooklyn Dodgers. The Dodgers, led by the fiery Leo (Lippy) Durocher, the man who was fond of saying, "Nice guys finish last," were to play in the World Series for the first time in twenty-one years.

Durocher, who had played shortstop for the Gas House Gang of St. Louis, had molded his club in the image of the rough-and-tough, give-no-quarter Cardinals of 1934. They were a fist-fighting, beanballing, cursing and spitting crew and no one, not even umpires, were safe from the rowdiest brand of ball the majors had ever witnessed. No skipper was thrown out of more games in the history of the diamond than ringleader Lippy, and Hugh Casey, the ace relief pitcher for the Dodgers, was once accused, not without reason, of trying to bean an umpire. Dodger spikes came high into second base every time there was a throw to that sack, especially when there was the possibility of breaking up a double play. The Scooter and Joe Gordon were not going to have an easy time of it.

The Yankees, of course, were ready to retaliate. They were just as tough as Durocher's gang, and they weren't going to be intimidated by the Dodgers' roughhouse tactics.

Every game of the Series proved to be a close one. The closer the game, the more intense the play and the greater the mayhem. As was expected, the greatest mayhem occurred around the midway sack.

The Dodgers started it by plowing into Gordon and Rizzuto, their base runners, spikes high, trying to cut down the shortstop and second baseman. The Yankees responded in kind, smashing into Peewee Reese and Billy Herman, then Pete Coscarart, who had come in to replace an injured Herman. Mickey Owen, the Dodger catcher, went ten feet out of the baseline to slide into the Scooter in a futile effort to break up a double play. Peewee Reese took a beating from hard-sliding, barreling Tommy Henrich, Charlie Keller, and Joe Gordon. It was hard-nosed baseball and every player was a target.

Then there was the beanball. There isn't a pitcher who doesn't throw a fast, inside ball, "the duster," to loosen up a hitter at the plate. The beanball, headed for a man's head, is something else. Too many players have had their heads cracked and their careers ended by a beanball. But Leo Durocher's pitchers were famous for it, especially their ace right-hander, Whitlow Wyatt. Wyatt threw a few too many close ones at Joe DiMaggio during the Series, and the usually quiet and mild-mannered DiMaggio came near to punching the pitcher out of the game. Wyatt and DiMaggio, both big men, squared off at the pitching mound. They glared at each other and said a few choice words. But, fortunately, the affair was broken up by teammates who rushed in to separate the two players. It was a rough, tough Series. It was also a well-played Series.

The two teams split the first two games, at Yankee Stadium, by the same scores, 3–2. Marius Russo, from the Scooter's old school, Richmond Hill High, won the third game, at Ebbets Field, 2–1, pitching against the Dodgers' knuckleballer Fat Fred Fitzsimmons, Hugh Casey, and two other relievers. In the fourth game, the Dodgers had a 4–3 lead going into the ninth inning and looked sure to tie the Series at 2 and 2.

Hugh Casey was pitching, and he retired the first two Yankee batters without any problem. One more out and Durocher's men would have their win. The Dodger fans were wild, anticipating a victory. They grew wilder and the noise in Ebbets Field was deafening as Casey, dealing to Tommy Henrich, ran the count to 3–2.

One more strike and it was all over, and Hugh Casey got that strike, as Tommy, fooled by a wide-breaking curve ball, took his cut and missed. But . . . sudden silence descended over the stands at Ebbets Field as the sure-handed Mickey Owen couldn't hold on to the ball, and there he was chasing the white pellet to the backstop as Tommy Henrich scooted down to first base.

Pandemonium. The special police fighting to keep the fans

in their seats and off the field. Cops pushing back Leo Durocher, who had run out onto the field, yelling at Owen to get
the ball.

When things quieted down again, there was Joe DiMaggio
standing at the plate and Hugh Casey so mad that all he could
throw was the fastball, and Joltin' Joe immediately lined the
pitch to left for a clean single, sending Tommy to third. Then
up came Charlie Keller with a double off the right field screen
to score Tommy and Joe that put the Yanks ahead, 5–4.

Why Durocher didn't call time-out so that Casey could settle down, or pull Casey from the game entirely, is still a matter
of conjecture. He was probably just as upset as his pitcher at
this point. In any case, Casey stayed on the mound, and the
Yanks went on to win that fourth game of the Series, 7–4.
Ernie Bonham pitched the final game of the championship,
defeating a dispirited Dodger club, 3–1. Once more, the New
York Yankees were champions of the baseball world.

It wasn't the best of World Series for the Scooter. He had
gotten only two hits, for a .111 average. However, he had
made eighteen assists and twelve putouts at short and compiled
a .968 fielding average. He would have better Series in the
years to come, though.

All things considered, he could look back on his first year in
the major leagues with considerable satisfaction. He was a
Yankee. He had proved himself worthy of the pinstripe uniform. He was, in everyone's opinion, one of the leading rookies in the game.

But the year wasn't quite over. There was the firemen's
banquet in Newark, and there was Cora. Especially, there
was Cora.

6

The Scooter in Love

The celebration of their World Series victory was just about over in the Yankees' dressing room. All the hollering, the back-slapping, the cork-popping, the champagne-drenching, all the usual rituals of the winning team were done with. Joe Di-Maggio was already in his street clothes, ready to go. As a matter of fact, he was in a hurry to go. The Scooter was just about ready, too.

"I've got to get to the airport," said Joe to the Scooter. "LaGuardia in Queens. Can you give me a lift?"

"Sure," said the Scooter, always ready to oblige.

"I've got to get to San Francisco," explained Joe.

"That's OK with me," said the Scooter.

Joe DiMaggio was a very private person. Phil was surprised he had told him as much as he did. He didn't ask him why he was in a hurry to get to San Francisco, especially with a Yankee victory celebration scheduled for that night at the Hotel Commodore in Manhattan. And Joe didn't tell him.

They were almost at LaGuardia before Joe spoke again.

"Say, Phil," he said, "I'm supposed to make a speech in Newark tomorrow night."

"I guess you won't be able to."

"No," Joe agreed. "It's their annual firemen's banquet. I sure hate to disappoint them."

"That's tough," said the Scooter, not expecting what was coming.

Joe was quiet for a moment, as if he were in deep thought, trying to figure some way out of his dilemma.

"Would you do it for me, Phil?" he asked abruptly, as if the idea had just occurred to him. "Go to the banquet for me?"

"Me?"

The Scooter was so surprised he almost let go of the steering wheel.

"Why not?"

"I can't speak at a banquet, Joe," he protested. "I've never been to a banquet, except at home, in my life! Besides, they're expecting Joe DiMaggio. I'm just Phil Rizzuto!"

"Then you'll do it?" said Joe.

The Scooter grinned, his small-boy, infectious grin. "So that's why you asked for the lift?"

"Never thought of it till just now," said Joe, his straight face giving no clue as to whether he was kidding or not.

"I hope they're not disappointed," the Scooter worried.

"They won't be," DiMaggio reassured him, as he left Phil for his flight to San Francisco.

Good-natured, always affable, the Scooter showed up at the banquet, and if the firemen were disappointed at not seeing Joe DiMaggio, they soon forgot about the Jolter, as the Scooter took the podium and began to talk baseball.

Phil always had a gift for telling a story. He was to realize it that night at the firemen's banquet, and it was a gift that would stand him in good stead for the years after he had hung up his glove and packed away his uniform. In fact, he was such a success at that firemen's banquet that, after the dinner and the autograph-signing session, the fire chief of Newark, Emil Esselborn, asked him to his house for a cup of coffee.

"It's too late, isn't it?" asked Phil.

"It's never too late in my house," responded the fire chief, "and I'd like my family to meet you. They're all baseball fans. They're all Yankee fans. You'll be giving them a treat."

Again, always obliging, Phil went along.

That visit to the fire chief's house was to bring about one of nature's more fortuitious meetings, and it was going to make for a most dramatic change in the life of the kid from Brooklyn.

They talked baseball all the way over to the house in the car. They talked baseball as Esselborn opened the front door and ushered Phil into his living room. Then Phil saw the fire chief's daughter, Cora, and, for a moment anyway, all the baseball talk stopped. Never did Cupid's arrow hit so sharply and so sure. The Scooter was in love.

Phil had never thought of girls much, and certainly not of love. His heart and soul belonged completely to baseball. There were pretty enough girls in the neighborhood, at Richmond Hill High School, and at the Roman Catholic Church on Myrtle Avenue where Phil attended mass every Sunday when he was home, to turn any young fellow's head, but not Phil's. It was all right for the other guys to meet and date the teenage beauties, but Phil couldn't see it for himself. Nothing, but nothing, would divert him from his one true love, baseball, not for a while anyway.

He had two sisters, and there were always girls dropping by the house and visiting, but "Hello" and "So long" were just about the extent of his conversation with them. And that was a lot, considering that he was just coming in after a game of baseball or running out to play one.

"He wasn't interested in parties," his mother said. "I don't think he ever had a date, when he was in school. At least, I don't remember any."

Of course Phil was shy and a bit conscious of his height. He continues to be shy, despite all the personal charm he shows today. It was this shyness, in addition to his trusting, gullible nature, that made him so lovable, and at the same time such an easy mark for all the pranks his teammates played on him.

But it was neither his shyness nor his self-consciousness that kept the Scooter, as a young man, away from the girls. It was the game, and only the game, which was on his mind every hour of the day and every day of the week.

"We had all we could do to get him to get dressed for church," said Mrs. Rizzuto. "Even before we got to breakfast, he was dressed in a uniform or a sweatshirt, and in his baseball shoes, ready to go out and play somewhere, anywhere. It was the same on all the Saints' Days and Easter, too. Baseball. Baseball. That's all that was ever on his mind."

Phil was eighteen years old when he left home to join the Class D baseball team in Bassett, Virginia. Away from home for the first time, and palling around with a bunch of other athletes, most of them older than he was, it wouldn't be hard to imagine the kid from Brooklyn kicking over a few cans, ripping up a few floors, heading pell-mell for all those pretty girls who are wild about baseball players. It didn't happen. Phil had a one-track mind, and that track went from one baseball station to another, with no side stops to slow it down.

It was the same way when Phil went up to Norfolk. No time for girls. No time for anything but baseball. When he got to

Kansas City, however, *amour* at long last came to the Scooter. Actually, it wasn't *amour*. It was more like the kind of love a kid of fourteen, fifteen, or perhaps sixteen experiences. "Puppy love" was what they used to call it.

She was a sweet, brown-haired girl named Betty Dresser. She was seventeen years old, and Phil not quite twenty. She came to the Kansas City games when the club was in town, and they would take walks together, sip sodas, take a ride in Phil's old car, and Betty would attend the games at Blues Stadium, but that was about it, except that Phil would occasionally have dinner at her home with her folks. The Dressers were very fond of Phil, as everybody was and would be, and they would have been glad to see this warm friendship between their daughter and the Scooter blossom into love and marriage. But it is doubtful that either of the kids had marriage in mind. Certainly Phil had no such thoughts at the time. He liked Betty well enough, liked being with her, but nothing, not even a sweetheart as lovely as Betty, could usurp baseball from first place in Phil's thinking, plans, or ambitions.

Of course there is no telling how that relationship between Betty Dresser and Phil Rizzuto may have developed. Many lifetime partnerships have had their start in friendships as innocent as Phil's and Betty's. Fate, unfortunately, stepped into the picture.

In 1940, while Phil was still playing for Kansas City, Betty Dresser went into the hospital for what was to be a simple tonsillectomy. Millions of people have tonsillectomies and walk out of the hospital hale and fit and in much better health as a result. Not Betty Dresser. A throat infection set in after surgery and Betty never recovered.

The tombstone on her grave carries her name, the date of

her birth, the date of her death, and the image of a baseball
player. The ballplayer looks a lot like Phil Rizzuto.

Phil was at the funeral, and he visited the grave again when
the Yankees played an exhibition game in Kansas City, in
1941. There wasn't another girl in young Phil Rizzuto's life
until after his first World Series.

But then, with one look at Cora Esselborn, the Scooter was
deeply, madly in love.

"The Kid" he called her.

"I saw the Kid," he says to this day, "and I guess my eyes
must have popped. I knew this was it. I went there for a cup of
coffee, and I was in love before I even got to the dining room."

And Cora, as she still says, was no less smitten that evening.

"I looked at him, a little dark-haired young man. He looked
at me. Believe it or not," she says, "I felt a thrill run up and
down my spine."

It was love at first sight. Whatever anyone says, it does
happen.

They started talking to each other right away, and not
about baseball. Fire chief Esselborn wanted to talk baseball
but he couldn't get a word in, up, down, or sideways. The kids
were too much involved with each other.

"That was a great Series," said Esselborn.

"Sure." Phil wasn't listening. He wasn't listening to anybody but Cora.

"Pretty rough," continued Esselborn.

"Yeah," said the Scooter.

"What if Owen hadn't dropped that third strike?"

"Sure," agreed Phil.

Esselborn gave up. He hadn't brought the Scooter home to
fall in love with his daughter, but there was nothing he could

do about it. Whatever the kids were going to talk about, it wasn't going to be baseball. He retired, and left the field to Cora and the Scooter.

Cora was indeed a very beautiful young lady. She could have been a model, if she had wanted to be one. She was to become, however, in the words of many an unbiased man and woman, the most beautiful wife in baseball. That night following the World Series, however, Cora Esselborn wasn't particularly interested in marriage. She was thinking of another career. She had studied at a Newark art school and was thinking seriously of becoming an illustrator of books and magazines.

It's hard to say why she fell so hard for the Scooter. She didn't know much about baseball and wasn't particularly interested in the game.

"I wasn't much interested in sports," she had said. "I knew there had been a World Series. You couldn't help knowing that in our house. My father ate up baseball. But the only baseball name I knew was Joe DiMaggio. I'd never even heard of Phil Rizzuto."

Whether she knew his name or not, she soon found herself having to hold back a love-stricken young Phil Rizzuto.

"Let's go out for a ride," suggested Phil. "We can stop for a coffee somewhere, or anything else you like."

Phil was eager. He had found the girl he wanted. He didn't want to let her go.

"It's a little late for that," said Cora.

Cora is Irish and Dutch. The Irish in her may account for her romantic strain. The Dutch part says, "Be practical, now. Be practical."

"There are lots of places open," persisted Phil.

"Not tonight."

"Come on!" insisted the Scooter.

Cora hesitated, the Irish fighting against the Dutch. The Dutch won out.

"I don't think a girl should go out with a fellow on the same night they meet," she said primly.

"Aw," said Phil, concealing nothing of his disappointment. Then, more brightly, "How about tomorrow night?"

Cora looked at her father, who had returned to the room and whose face was buried in the sports page of his newspaper.

She turned to Phil and smiled.

"All right," she agreed. "Tomorrow night."

Phil didn't want to wait till tomorrow night. He didn't even want to leave.

"I just wanted to be with Cora," he said. "I wanted to be with her all the time."

It wasn't until well after midnight that he was ushered out of the Esselborn house. He was floating on air. He got into his car, his every thought about Cora. He couldn't drive home to Long Island. Long Island was too far away from Cora. He drove to the Douglas Hotel in Newark and got himself a room. And he didn't get much sleep that night, thinking of the beautiful girl he had just met. For once, the Scooter had forgotten about baseball. Fortunately, baseball was over for the year.

He picked up Cora the next night. They went out for a ride. They stopped for coffee at the nicest place he could find. Then they went riding some more.

Late, as late as he could manage, the Scooter brought the girl home, then rushed back to his hotel, picked up the phone, and dialed.

"Cora? This is Phil!"

And they talked for hours.

For some thirty days after, the routine was the same. Phil called for Cora every night. They went for a ride in his car. They stopped for coffee or a Coke. He took her home, rushed back to his hotel, picked up the phone, dialed, and they stayed on the phone for another three hours.

One night at the end of that hectic month, sitting in a roadside cafe, Cora was a bit more thoughtful than usual.

Phil sensed that things weren't quite as right as they'd been. "Something wrong, Cora?" he asked.

Cora looked into the Scooter's boyish eyes. She really loved him, but she was afraid things were happening too fast.

"This thing is getting too serious, Phil," she said.

"What do you mean, too serious?" the Scooter almost yelled. "I want to marry you!"

There! He'd said it!

"I know," said Cora, quietly, but Cora was a very practical young lady. "But are we really in love, Phil?" she asked.

Phil could answer for himself, but not for Cora.

"I think we ought not to see each other for a while," said Cora. "Let's see how we feel after we've been apart for a while."

"I couldn't stay away from you," protested Phil.

"You'll have to," insisted Cora. "That's the way I want it. Go out of town for a while. We'll both know better then, we'll know for sure, if we really love each other."

The Scooter was crestfallen, but Cora had made up her mind and all his pleading could do nothing to change it. He went out of town. He went all the way down to Norfolk, Virginia, where he had friends and shoulders to cry on.

Phil had been in Norfolk only a few weeks, fretting and worrying about Cora and feeling sorry for himself, when the

Japanese pulled their sneak attack on Pearl Harbor, catapulting the United States into the Second World War. The date was December 7, 1941, a day, as President Franklin Delano Roosevelt called it in his broadcast to the nation, "that would live in infamy."

That night, Lefty Gomez, always the prankster, called Phil's mother.

"Mrs. Rizzuto, where's Phil?"

"In Norfolk."

"Tell him to take the next train and come home. The Japs are going to land in New York and we need everybody we can get to defend Yankee Stadium."

Mrs. Rizzuto knew that Lefty was just making another one of his jokes, but the attack on Pearl Harbor had everyone concerned. No one knew what was going to happen next, and a Japanese attack on New York was not beyond possibility.

She called Phil, delivered Lefty Gomez's message, and the Scooter was on the very next train out of Norfolk. It wasn't the Japanese he was worried about; it was the hope that he would be able to see Cora again that had him moving so fast.

As soon as he landed in New York, he called her. He told her about the call Lefty Gomez had made to his mother.

"But that's not the reason I'm back here," he said. "I came back because I want to see you."

Cora was delighted to see him again, and Phil was the happiest kid in town. They began talking about marriage.

The drafting of young men into the armed forces of the United States had been in full swing for almost two years. The Glendale draft board had classified the Scooter as 3A. This was the classification for men who were the sole support of families, and Phil was the sole support of his parents. His father was earning very little, working part-time. His brother was unemployed.

"I'd like to play one more year for the Yankees," he told Cora. "I'd like to earn enough money so that my mother and father will have enough to live on while I'm in the service."

It meant postponing their wedding date, but Cora, always level-headed, was in full agreement with the Scooter.

They saw a good deal of each other during the winter, up to the time Phil left for spring training. Then it was all baseball and not nearly enough of Cora for the Scooter.

"It just wasn't possible," said a rueful Phil. "We were on the road half the time, and when we were playing at home, I had to be home early and stay in shape."

The Scooter's batting average slipped a bit in the 1942 season, to .284, but his fielding was more brilliant than ever. He led American League shortstops in participating in double plays, as he had in 1941, and on August 14 he tied a major league record by participating in five double plays in one game. And he led shortstops in the American League with 324 putouts. All this, despite the fact that he played ball for more than three weeks with a concussion.

Toward the end of July 1942, the Detroit Tigers' Billy Hitchcock—the same Billy Hitchcock who had given Phil his nickname—kicked the Scooter in the head, accidentally, sliding into second base. A couple of days later, the Scooter landed on his head, colliding with a White Sox pitcher. The pitcher was covering first, and Phil was trying to beat out a bunt.

Those two accidents hurt, but the Scooter never left the lineup. He did suffer an awful lot of headaches, however, and the vision of his left eye was blurred. To add to his woes, he lost his appetite, and he couldn't fall asleep at night, either. But he kept on playing, still making those impossible plays at shortstop, working like a well-oiled machine in those double plays.

Before a game one day Phil mentioned the troubles he was having to Joe Gordon. He was afraid to talk to Joe McCarthy, afraid the skipper might pull him out of the game.

"Better see the doctor," advised Gordon and, reluctantly, the Scooter paid a visit to Dr. Robert Emmett Walsh, the Yankees' physician at the time.

The doctor took X rays of Phil's head and examined them carefully.

"Concussion," said the doctor.

"Holy cow!" exclaimed the Scooter.

"And you've been playing all this time?" asked Walsh.

"Yeah," said Scooter. "Didn't seem to bother me."

No one would have guessed, watching Rizzuto, that he was playing with a concussion, and he never missed a game. He was all over the field and played brilliantly.

The Yankees lost the World Series to a hustling, scrapping, hungry bunch of St. Louis Cardinals, winning only one game in the autumn classic. That was the year Billy Southworth managed the Cardinals and the team boasted such knock-'em-down, drag-'em-out players like Enos Slaughter, Stan Musial, Terry Moore, Mort Cooper, Johnny Beazley, and Whitey Kurowski.

Still, it was a marvelous year for Phil Rizzuto, despite the concussion. He topped off the season with the best World Series batting average for the Yankees, slugging the ball at a .381 clip. In the fifth and final game of the Series, Phil led off the first inning and stepped in to hit against Johnny Beazley. Beazley came in with his fast ball and Phil took his best cut— a terrific swing—caught the ball on the fat part of the bat, and drove it over the left field fence for a home run. It was his first World Series home run, and he was ecstatic. But the Yankees went down 4–2 as the Cards took the game and Series.

It wasn't the happiest of times for the New York Yankees, but there were other things, and perhaps more important things, on the minds of the players in 1942. There was a war to be won, and the war needed men. The ranks of the major leagues had already begun to be thinned by the ballplayers' exchanging their baseball suits for the uniforms of the United States armed forces. Of all the men on big league rosters on December 7, 1941, more than half would enlist in the service of their country. Phil Rizzuto would be among them.

7

You're in
the Navy Now!

The Scooter knew that his 3A draft classification wasn't going to last forever. Besides, he didn't feel good, as a young fellow in top physical condition, playing ball when all the other boys were marching off to fight for Uncle Sam.

Fred Hutchinson, the Detroit pitcher, suggested to the Scooter that, if he applied in time, he could be stationed at the U.S. Navy Training Station in Norfolk, Virginia. The idea appealed to the Scooter. Bob Feller, the all-time great pitcher, and Hutchinson, as well as a number of other ballplayers, were already stationed there. Phil had a good number of friends in Norfolk, too. Besides, Phil didn't like the possibility of his being drafted into the Army, and the Air Force didn't appeal to him much—Phil had a fear of flying.

The Scooter talked it over with Cora and with his folks.

"Norfolk isn't that far from Newark," he said to Cora. "There'll be weekend passes and stuff. We don't need to be so far apart."

As for his folks, Phil had managed to put away enough money to keep them comfortable, and no one figured the war was going to last long.

66

These details attended to, early in August of 1942 Phil asked Joe McCarthy for a couple of days off.

"If I enlist now," he explained to Joe, "they'll give me a couple of months before I report for duty. At least that's what they tell me."

And that's the way things worked out. Phil took the train to Norfolk, passed the physical, as might have been expected, was sworn in, and was granted permission to report for active duty on October 7, 1942. That gave him all the time he needed to finish the year with the Yankees and play in the World Series. It would be a long time before the Scooter would get back in pinstripes.

For eight weeks, Phil went through boot camp at Norfolk, like every other recruit in the Navy. Like every other recruit, he wore the bell-bottom trousers, middie blouse, and white hat of the apprentice seaman. But, unlike the other recruits, the Scooter was a baseball star. And to all the young sailors in boot camp, his life was touched with glamor.

"What's Joe DiMaggio really like?"

"Is Lefty Gomez as crazy as they say he is?"

"How do you think Crosetti is going to make out, playing short again?"

"What happened to the Yankees in the World Series?"

"How did you feel when you got that home run?"

There were few kids in the Navy who weren't baseball fans. And they pumped the Scooter for every bit of inside information they could get out of him. Needless to say, the Scooter loved all the attention. If he wasn't playing baseball, he could talk about it, and for hour after hour he entranced his eager audience with his endless fund of stories about the men who played ball and about the game itself.

Understandably, the Scooter was perhaps the most popular recruit in boot camp, and there can be no doubt that he loved being in the limelight. But he missed Cora, missed her more than he ever thought he would.

He called her every chance he could get.

"I wish you were here, Cora," he would say plaintively over the telephone. "I want to see you so badly. It's so lonely down here.

"I'll be getting some leave after boot camp," Phil went on. "Maybe we can get married then, and you could come down here and we'd get a house near the base somewhere."

Cora wasn't sure about that.

"I'll be through with boot in January," pressed Phil. "We can get married in January, can't we, Cora?"

"Let me think about it," said Cora.

"Please," pleaded the Scooter. "I know you'll like it here. I've got a lot of friends here. You'll like them. I'll call you tomorrow, Cora."

He called every day and Cora finally agreed to get married, but not in January, in June.

"June? That far off?"

"It's only a few months," Cora consoled.

It seemed more like an eternity for the Scooter, but Cora had set the date and she wasn't going to change her mind. Phil just had to be patient. That's about all he could do. Cora Esselborn had a mind of her own, and the Scooter was going to have to live with it.

Actually, things weren't that rough on the Scooter, and, as he had told Cora, he had plenty of friends at the Navy base. There was Fred Hutchinson, Bob Feller, and Dom DiMaggio, Joe DiMaggio's brother, an outfielder with the Boston Red

Sox before he enlisted. There was Don Padgett, who had played for the St. Louis Cardinals; Benny McCoy, who had played for the Philadephia Athletics; Hugh Casey and Peewee Reese of the Dodgers; the slugging Sam Chapman of the Philadelphia A's; Eddie Robinson of the Cleveland Indians; and Pittsburgh Pirate catcher Vinnie Smith. And there was the sportswriter Morris Segal. These were all pals of the Scooter, all attached to the Norfolk Training Station athletic program, and there were also a number of professional boxers and basketball players.

In the spring of 1943, they would all be playing baseball as members of the Norfolk Training Station team. The program, devised by the Navy brass, was intended as a morale builder. The games, arranged between teams from different camps, were watched by thousands of service men, some recruits, some about to embark for combat, some veterans returned from Pearl Harbor, Guadalcanal, the Philippines, Midway, New Guinea, and other fierce and bloody spots on the globe.

The games were a real treat for all the sailors. If only for a few hours, it broke the monotony of basic training, of their daily duties around camp, of the grim realities of war. It was the contention of the Navy brass that these games were as valuable to morale as the USO shows, the personal appearances of movie and theater stars, and movies.

Stan Musial of the St. Louis Cardinals and Dick Sisler, who would join the Cards in 1946, came down with the Bainbridge, Maryland, Naval Station squad to play against the Norfolk team. The great Ted Williams and Buddy Hassett, who had played first base for the Yankees in 1942, came up with another service team to play the Norfolk men. There were others, and occasionally a major league team came to Norfolk during spring training, or even during the regular season, to play against the Navy boys. Once, the Norfolk nine traveled to Washington, D.C., to hand the Senators a good licking. Tickets for that game were purchased by buying war bonds ranging in price from one-hundred to twenty-five thousand dollars, and in the end nearly three million dollars in bonds were sold.

Baseball was a morale builder, all right, and no one was happier playing the game than the Scooter. If nothing else, it made that long wait for June and his marriage to Cora just a little less painful.

Finally, the day of the wedding approached. Phil had arranged for a day off from camp on June 23. He had received permission for the leave from Gary Brodie, the coach of the Norfolk baseball squad. Brodie was a career Navy man, a chief boatswain. He was all Navy, a stickler for the rules. Everything had to be done and carried out according to Navy regulations, and Brodie was tough enough to see that these regulations were followed to the letter, no matter who it was that had to follow them. And once he had made up his mind, it seemed that nothing could change it.

On June 22, one day before Phil's scheduled leave to get married, the Norfolk Training team had a miserable day in the field against the Norfolk Naval Air Station and lost badly. Brodie was up in arms. He railed at his charges in what might be called typical Navy fashion and immediately arranged for a doubleheader with the Air men for the next day, June 23, the Scooter's wedding day; and no one on the team was excused from duty for those games.

"That's my day off," protested the Scooter. "I'm getting

married tomorrow. You said I could have the day off."

Brodie might as well have not been listening.

"There's a doubleheader tomorrow," he barked. "Every one of you guys better be here to play it."

"But . . . ," began the Scooter.

He never finished.

"That's final!" snapped Brodie, and he walked off, leaving Phil completely bewildered.

For a moment Phil thought it might be a gag. They were always pulling stunts on him at the base. But this was no gag. He had already reserved the church for the wedding. He had arranged for a priest to perform the ceremony. He had rented a parlor at the Monticello Hotel in Norfolk for the reception. He had a honeymoon suite reserved at a hotel in Virginia Beach. Cora and all the relatives on both sides of the family were on their way from New York for the nuptials and the celebration. He wanted to tell Boatswain Brodie but Brodie wasn't listening.

But Dom DiMaggio was listening, and he wasn't going to let Phil Rizzuto be handed such a raw deal. There wasn't much time to get things straightened out, so Dom acted quickly and with a good deal of anger.

He found Brodie and, without wasting any words, laid down an ultimatum to the coach.

"If Phil Rizzuto doesn't get the day off for his wedding," he said sharply, "there won't be a game tomorrow."

"What do you mean?" demanded Brodie, his dander up at this display of insubordination. Insubordination is not looked on kindly by regular Navy men.

"I mean that I won't play," said Dom, angry enough not to be frightened by the menacing tones of his superior. "And neither will anyone else. We'll strike if you make Rizzuto show up here tomorrow." ·

"Strike!" bellowed Brodie.

He had never heard the word in the Navy before.

"I'll have you all court-martialed! I'll have you all sent out on sea duty!"

"You do what you like," Dom retorted. "There's nothing in regulations says we have to play baseball. Send me to sea. I liked it in San Francisco on the small-boat detail I had. The Navy brought me here to play ball. I didn't ask for it! Same goes for all of us! Where's the rule that we have to play baseball? Show it to me!"

Brodie backed down. DiMaggio was right. There was no rule that a Navy man had to play baseball. The twin bill with the Air Station was rescheduled. The Scooter got the day off to get married.

No one could have asked for a better friend than Dom DiMaggio. He certainly had saved the day for the Scooter. But that good deed wasn't going to stop him from playing a trick on the little guy. No one stopped playing tricks on Rizzuto.

Phil and Cora were married, as scheduled, in a small Catholic Church near the training base on the afternoon of June 23, 1943, Cora in a beautiful bridal gown, the Scooter in his middie blouse and bell-bottom trousers. The Scooter was one happy fellow, surrounded by both families and the ballplayers, and his other friends from the base, and with his radiant bride on his arm.

From the church, the whole party moved to the Monticello Hotel for the reception. There was plenty to eat, plenty to drink, and an almost endless repetition of toasts and good wishes for the bride and groom.

Eventually, Phil began to look forward to getting away from the crowd to that honeymoon suite where he could be alone with Cora. But before he could leave, a few of his pals quietly slipped away, their plan known only to them.

Having escaped the reception, Dom DiMaggio, with Don Padgett, Benny McCoy, and Morris Segal, headed for the Cavalier Hotel in Virginia Beach, where the Scooter had reserved the honeymoon suite.

Dom took off the glasses he wore and walked up to the registration desk.

"I'm Phil Rizzuto," he announced to the hotel clerk. "Have you got the suite I reserved ready?"

The clerk wasn't a baseball fan. The reservation had been made over the phone, and the clerk wouldn't have known Phil Rizzuto from Babe Ruth. But he did know that Phil had been married that afternoon. He'd read it in the local newspaper.

"Yes, Mr. Rizzuto," said the clerk to Dom DiMaggio. "The suite's ready, but where's your bride?"

Dom was prepared for that question.

"She'll be coming in a while," he said. "You know those Italian weddings. There's all that crying and all those good-byes. I just want to check the suite, see if everything is all right."

"Oh, everything will be all right, Mr. Rizzuto," said the clerk, completely sold on Dom's story, and he gave DiMaggio the key to the suite and pointed out the hotel elevator to him.

Dom got into the elevator and was quickly joined by Padgett, McCoy, and Segal, who had walked quietly through the hotel lobby.

Once in the suite, they hurriedly set up a table and four

chairs. McCoy had a deck of cards, and they began to play a game of hearts, expecting the arrival of Phil and Cora momentarily. But the groom and his bride ran into an extraordinary roadblock, and the wait was longer than any of the card players had expected.

It was an Italian wedding all right, as DiMaggio had explained to the hotel clerk, but it wasn't tears and good-byes that held up the newlyweds. It was an air-raid drill, ordered by the Army, which was indifferent to the newly married couple's desire to be alone. All through the war there were these drills, and all without any warning to the general public or the civilian air-raid wardens.

Phil and Cora had already said their good-byes, received all the good wishes, run the gauntlet of rice hurlers, and were on the way to the hotel in the Scooter's Model A Ford, when the sirens began to wail, and an air-raid warden stepped into the middle of the road to stop them.

For a moment Phil thought his pals might be pulling one of their stunts on him, but the civilian air-raid warden quickly convinced him that it was the real thing, an air-raid drill ordered by the Army.

"You'll just have to stay where you are, young fellow, until we get the all-clear signal," said the warden.

"Just what we need," said Phil, under his breath.

"What's that?" asked the civilian.

"Nothing," said Phil.

Cora was crying. All the excitement of the wedding and the reception, and now the wailing of the air-raid sirens, were just a little too much for her.

"It won't take long, ma'am," said the kindly warden. "Do you mind if I sit with you until we get the all-clear?"

Cora moved closer to Phil. She felt more comfortable that way. And the air-raid warden sat with them for what seemed like hours to the Scooter, until the blessed all-clear finally sounded.

They finally did get to the Virginia Beach hotel. There was another clerk on duty at the desk and there was no difficulty in getting the key to the suite Phil had reserved. They took the elevator to their rooms, walked to the door of the suite, and opened it.

"What's this!" yelled Phil.

All the lights were on and there were four of his pals playing cards in the middle of the room.

No one answered. The four pals continued their game.

Finally, when the deal was over, they politely turned their heads to the newlyweds and said, just as politely, "Good evening." Then they resumed their game.

"Come on, you guys," pleaded the Scooter. "A joke's a joke, but this is going too far."

He might as well have been speaking to the fixtures in the room. The four pals just continued to shuffle the cards, deal, and play. No matter how much Phil begged them to go, they just weren't going.

Phil sat down on the couch, completely frustrated. Cora sat down next to him. Here they were, just married, and all they could do was to sit together on the couch, hold hands, and look at each other.

The Scooter asked Cora whether she would like some coffee.

"Order some for us, too," said McCoy, without interrupting his game.

Phil shrugged his shoulders, and ordered coffee for all of them. When the coffee arrived, the four pals took theirs at the table and, without as much as a word to either Phil or Cora, continued to play the cards in their hands.

They sat at that table for another hour or more before they got tired of the game and felt that they had worked the gag long enough. Only then did they rise from their seats.

"Thanks for the room," said each of the Scooter's pals in turn, and finally they left the bride and groom alone.

8

The Series, Military-Style

Ted Williams and the ballplayers of the NC Pre-Flight Base were at Norfolk for a scheduled ballgame, but before the players could take the field for pregame practice, a sudden storm hit the camp. There would be no game that afternoon. The boys just sat around the locker room chewing the fat.

The talk was all baseball, of course—how the men felt about the major leagues with half the big leaguers in the Armed Forces, and general chitchat about certain games, clutch hits, odd-balls in the game, and so forth.

Phil told them about the first game he ever played in the majors, opening day of the 1941 season in Washington, D.C., and about the thrill he had had when Franklin Delano Roosevelt tossed out the first ball. Then there were the girls who had come up from Norfolk with a load of presents for him. He had a story about Lefty Gomez, too.

"We were playing the Dodgers in Yankee Stadium, an exhibition game in April. Lefty was pitching, and all of a sudden those Brooklyn Bums began to tee off on him. The base hits were just rattling all over the place.

"Lefty didn't seem to be fazed at all. He took a look at me

at short. I was a bit nervous, and I guess I was shoving the dirt around with my feet.

He called me over to the mound.

" 'What are you so jittery about?' he asked me.

" 'Go ahead and pitch,' I said.

" 'Are you nervous because your mother's in the box, watching you?' he asked.

"I didn't answer that one," said Phil, going on with his story, "but he played it to the hilt.

" 'Well, stick around, kid,' Gomez says to me. 'Stick around and talk to me. Shake your head and pretend you're mad because I'm answering back. Your ma will sure be proud.'

"I asked Gomez why that would make my mother proud.

" 'You dope!' said Gomez. 'When she sees her son telling the great Gomez how to pitch, she'll know he's finally made the Yankees.' "

"I told him to go soak his head," said Phil, and the ball-players, sitting in the locker room, out of the rain, had a good laugh.

Phil also told them about the time he drove his ten-year-old Ford, a convertible, into the Yankee Stadium parking lot.

"It was a beat-up old thing. No windshield, the canvas top torn in ribbons, pinup pictures of movie stars pasted on the dashboard, fur tails flying from the hood.

"There was only one parking spot when I got there, right between Ruffing's Cadillac and Gomez's La Salle. Someone must have told Ed Barrow about it, and he really gave it to me.

" 'That thing looks terrible out there,' he snapped at me. 'Get it out of there and don't let me ever see it again. Don't you realize that you are a big leaguer with the Yankees, young man?'

"I was scared. I never did drive that car again to Yankee

Stadium. I should have asked him for the money to buy a better car," said Phil, "but I was too dumb then. I'd know better now."

The guys liked that story, too, but they had had enough stories; they had other ideas about how to pass the hours on this rainy day. As a matter of fact, everyone in the locker room was in on the stunt, except the Scooter; he had no forewarning of what was in store for him.

Ted Williams flashed a prearranged signal, and suddenly Williams, Fred Hutchinson, Benny McCoy, and a few others jumped up from their seats and pinned the Scooter to the wall. They took off his shoes and socks. They took off his bell-bottom trousers, his middie blouse, and every other stitch of clothing he was wearing. Four of the boys pinned him down and Ted Williams produced a bottle of indelible red mercury solution.

"Oh, no!" pleaded the Scooter.

They weren't listening.

The solution Ted Williams had was used to protect the skin before adhesive tape was put on some scratch, cut, wound of any kind. It prevented the skin from peeling when the tape was removed. And Ted was an artist at applying the solution to the body.

"I love you, Cora," he printed on the Scooter's chest. "I'm a Naval hero," he painted on another part of the Scooter's anatomy. He printed a lot of other things that were somewhat less pretty, and needn't be mentioned, all over his victim's body. And there was no way Phil could remove all that indelible red mercury solution. It would just have to wear away with time —two, three days, maybe a week.

Phil and Cora were living in a little place off the Navy base at the time. He'd get up in the morning and ride his Model A Ford to camp, and hurry back home as soon as he could, making fast tracks to his beautiful, loving wife. But, that rainy afternoon, he lingered in camp a bit. He didn't know how Cora would react to the shennanigans of the sailors that rainy day—to that red stuff all over his body and the things Ted Williams had printed on it.

He needn't have been so worried, however. Cora had heard enough stories about the gags that had been pulled on her gentle and forgiving husband. She took one look at all that red stuff and couldn't help laughing at Phil's body tattoo. She knew that everyone loved her little guy—that there was no malice in the gags—and she took the red messages on poor Phil's body in stride, just as she would take all the gags pulled on the Scooter.

One time, Fred Hutchinson and Vinnie Smith turned the Scooter's Model A car upside down, where it was parked near the ballfield. Phil had a time of it putting that Ford right-side up.

Once in a while, they'd find the key to the old car in the Scooter's pants in the locker room, then drive the car on to the ballfield and right into the dugout, with all the ballplayers scattering for safety. Sometimes they would turn the car on the Scooter himself, chasing him all over the diamond, as if they really meant to run him over.

"I had to climb the backstop screen," said Phil, "or dive into a hole under the bleachers to get away from those maniacs."

And there were the other gags, like tearing up his underwear, or nailing his shoes to the ground, or throwing him into the shower with all his clothes on; there was even the time that the fellows got Bob Johnson, in camp with the Washington Senators, to rip the roof off the Scooter's Ford with his bare hands. It cost Phil ten dollars to get that roof fixed. But all the tomfoolery came to an abrupt end when Phil and all his pals were shipped out to sea, for armed combat, early in January 1944.

"I'll never forget the day they told me I was going overseas," says the Scooter. "I'd done nothing but play ball all the time I was in the Navy. I was in no way prepared for any kind of combat, and they put me in charge of a twenty-millimeter gun crew! On a ship!

"They gave us a duffle bag with a rifle in it. I didn't know anything about rifles. I didn't know the first thing about shooting a gun."

Nevertheless, Phil was put in charge of a twenty-millimeter gun crew and shipped off to the receiving station at Gammadodo in New Guinea. There he was given Atabrine pills, a preventive medication for malaria.

"Those pills are going to make you turn yellow," said a couple of the Navy men stationed with him in New Guinea.

"Yeah?" said Phil. "I'm not going to turn yellow," and he didn't take the pills.

As a result, he came down with malaria. He also got a fungus infection and the shingles, an extremely painful disease. And then he was always seasick, to boot.

"The minute I got up on my feet, in the boat, my stomach would go," said Phil. "I'd get violently ill."

He'd lie down and try to get rid of his miseries, but the captain of the ship wouldn't let him.

"Rizzuto, get your gun crew out."

As leader of the gun crew, Rizzuto was supposed to spot the

planes that flew over the ship and identify them as American or Canadian or Japanese.

"But they came over so fast," said Phil. "They flew so fast and so low that you didn't know who they were.

"You know," he continued, "if we had had more men like me in the service, we would have lost the war."

The Scooter said he was threatened with court-martial because he wasn't able to perform his duties. It wasn't that he didn't want to follow orders; he just couldn't. He was too ill with malaria.

Almost everybody got malaria in the Pacific, but Phil had it bad. It was so bad that they shipped him to a hospital in Brisbane, Australia.

At the hospital, he followed doctor's orders and took every kind of medicine that was given him without question. He also followed the diet prescribed: milk, eggs, and steak. Slowly, gradually, but certainly, the Scooter got better and regained the strength the malaria had cost him. Commander George Halas, the great coach and owner of the Chicago Bears at the time, was in charge of the Navy's athletic program in Brisbane. He assigned the Scooter the job of supervising the physical rehabilitation program for Navy men who were recuperating from illnesses or wounds. Phil was also assigned the job of helping to organize programs of sports and games for those Navy men who were well enough to play.

Except for his participation in the games he set up for the convalescents, Phil didn't get to play any ball in Australia. He did get into one game, or rather a series of games in Hawaii, and that's another story.

There were a good many major league ballplayers stationed by the Army in Hawaii in the summer of 1944. Joe

DiMaggio was there. So were Joe Gordon, Red Ruffing, and Johnny Beazley. Jerry Priddy, the Scooter's old pal who had been traded to the Washington Senators after the 1942 season, was there, too.

The Navy had a number of ballplayers stationed in Hawaii, as well, but not of the caliber of DiMaggio, Gordon, and Ruffing, and the Army brass didn't bother to conceal the contempt it had for the Navy men.

Admiral Nimitz, the Navy's top admiral, and one of our great war heroes, wasn't very happy about the situation. Like all good Navy men he thought that anything the Army could do, the Navy could do better. He gathered all the major league players who were posted at Naval stations in Australia and the States and had them shipped to the Pacific islands, then challenged the Army to a World Series—a World Series between the Army and the Navy.

By September 1944, Navy men Virgil Trucks, Peewee Reese, Johnny Mize, Hugh Casey, Johnny Vander Meer, Walt Masterson, and Al Brancato were in Hawaii. The Scooter and Dom DiMaggio, both stationed in Australia, boarded a plane for Honolulu, bumping a couple of sailors who were headed home on furlough after months in some of the hottest battles of the war.

Phil felt pretty rotten about bumping those two boys from the plane.

"These kids have been fighting and we're just a couple of ballplayers. It's a bum deal," he said, showing his usual sensitivity to the feelings of others and a proper sense of justice.

Of course he had no say in the matter. A Navy man follows orders.

The enlisted men and women, both Army and Navy, and

their officers, showed a wild enthusiasm for the service World
Series. Everyone in the Armed Forces was eager to get to the
games. Unofficially, thousands of dollars were bet on both
teams. Originally the Series was scheduled for seven games,
but the demand for tickets was so great that the Series was
extended to eleven games.

The service Series opened with all the ceremony and hoopla
of the major leagues' fall classic, with color guards, a benedic-
tion by a clergyman (in military uniform), and the traditional
tossing out of the first ball. At Furlong Stadium on the
grounds of the Schofield Army barracks in Honolulu, it was
Admiral Nimitz who had the honor of delivering the cere-
monial first pitch. But, before doing so, he had a few words for
all the cheering servicemen and servicewomen in the stands.

"We are all in a bigger league," was one of the phrases he
used. "We plan to keep the Japs in the cellar until they learn to
play ball with civilized nations."

He spoke in the language of baseball—a language all
Americans know—to a thunderous roar of approval. Then
he tossed out the ball to an even greater roar of approval.

Yankee catcher Bill Dickey, a lieutenant in the Navy, was
the manager of the Navy team. He had the slugging Johnny
Mize at first base. He put Peewee Reese at shortstop, so that
the partisan Brooklyn Dodger fans wouldn't raise a ruckus.
He had the Scooter play third, and Phil was glad to play any
position on the diamond, just so he was playing ball. Among
others he had Joe Grace, outfielder for the St. Louis Browns in
peace time; Barney McCosky, another outfielder, of the Detroit Tigers; and a truly great pitching staff, including Johnny
Vander Meer, who had pitched two successive no-hit games
for the Cincinnati Reds back in 1938, Virgil Trucks of the

Detroit Tigers, former Tiger Schoolboy Rowe, and the Dodger fire-baller Hugh Casey. It was a team that was going to prove too much for the Army, particularly since its biggest star, Joe DiMaggio, was out with ulcers.

Johnny Beazley pitched the first game for the Army. Virgil Trucks was on the mound for the Navy, and he had the Army men completely helpless at the plate. The Army couldn't get anything started against the Detroit pitcher, and Navy walked off the field that first afternoon of the World Series with a 5–0 victory.

Johnny Vander Meer and Hugh Casey shared the honors for the men in blue in the second game of the set-to, and they were almost as good as Trucks had been the day before. Joe Grace belted a grand-slam home run, and Navy made it two in a row with an 8–2 win.

As a matter of fact, Navy won the first five games of that series before giving one up to the Army.

Surveying the scene, a very satisfied Admiral Nimitz was all smiles.

"It only goes to prove what I've been saying all along," he declared, medals gleaming on his chest. "No one tops the Navy."

Certainly the Army didn't in those games in Honolulu. When all the hitting and running was over, Navy had taken eight of the eleven games of the World Series, Army two. One game, called because of a tremendous storm, ended in a tie score.

"We sure demoralized the Army," boasted Virgil Trucks, recalling that crucial meeting between the two service baseball teams.

Phil Rizzuto played brilliant and errorless ball in the field and did well at the plate, collecting twelve hits. As a matter of fact, the Scooter had such a good time in Hawaii that he even tried to get transferred to the islands. His request for transfer, however, along with a dozen other similar ones, was denied. Immediately after the games, the Navy men were returned to the posts from which they had been plucked to play ball. The Scooter was shipped back, along with Dom DiMaggio, to Australia.

The Americans had been pushing the Japanese back in the Pacific. The fighting was moving west toward the Philippines. The Scooter was sent to Finschhafen in New Guinea. Two months in Finschhafen and Phil was promoted to Specialist, First Class, and assigned to the SS *Triangulum*. The *Triangulum* was a Cargo ship that carried supplies from New Guinea to the southwest Pacific island of Manus. The Scooter was in charge of a crew on a twenty-millimeter antiaircraft gun but saw very little action.

"Once in a while," he said, "a Jap plane would come in sight and we'd take a few shots at it, but we never hit any."

The Scooter had gotten his sea legs by this time and his stomach could take the sea roll, but the stint was boring, and, after three months on the *Triangulum*, the Scooter was glad to be transferred to shore duty once again, at Samar, another island in the Philippines.

It was January 1945. The Japanese had been cleared out of the Philippines by this time and the Americans were heading for the bloody battles of Iwo Jima and Okinawa. On Samar, the Scooter was promoted again, this time to chief petty officer, and was again administering an athletic program, organizing boxing matches, handball tournaments, and softball games. He was responsible, too, for supervising the other recreational activities on the island.

Early in August 1945, the United States dropped an atomic bomb on Hiroshima, Japan. It was the first time an A-bomb had been employed in warfare. The explosive force of that bomb was equivalent to 12,500 tons of TNT. The number of lives it took and the damage it created were enormous.

A couple of days after Hiroshima, the United States dropped a second A-bomb, this time on Nagasaki.

The use of the A-bombs was intended to bring the war to a quick finish, and that much was accomplished. Japan surrendered, unconditionally, in August. The fighting, the killing was all over, and the millions of men who were still in the Pacific would soon be heading home. They were more than ready and eager for the journey back to the States, to their sisters and brothers, their mothers and fathers, their sweethearts, wives, and children. The Scooter had a special reason to want to hurry back home.

Many a serviceman had had word, while on duty in the Pacific, that his wife had given him a son or a daughter. Some of those men never saw the children who bore their names; they had lost their lives in the fighting, were buried on land or at sea, and never came home.

But Phil was going home, not only to his beautiful wife Cora, but to a beautiful little daughter as well.

On March 8, 1944, Cora gave birth to their first child at the Presbyterian Hospital in Newark. The girl was named Patricia Ann. Phil was in Australia at the time, and the Navy wasn't giving leaves to sailors to go see their first-born or whatever-born. Cora sent pictures, of course, and all the little details that make the first months and years of a child's life so dear and precious to its parents. But words and pictures are never the same as being right there, on the spot, to witness the miracles. Phil wasn't there to hear little Patti say "Mama" or

"Papa" for the first time, to watch her crawl, to take her first hesitant and wobbly steps.

Patti would be twenty months old before the Scooter saw his daughter. He was returned to the States on a transport that docked at San Jose, California, in mid-October. First thing, like almost all the other boys and men, he rushed for the telephone.

"Cora! I'm home!"

Well, not exactly.

There was the flight to Camp Shelton in Norfolk, and only then, after more than three years as a sailor, after nineteen months overseas, was Phil Rizzuto released from the United States Navy.

On October 28, 1945, the Scooter doffed his middie blouse, white cap, and bell-bottom trousers. The war was over and Phil Rizzuto once more was a civilian.

9

Back in Pinstripes

In 1945, while the war was still on, the heirs of Colonel Jacob Ruppert, owners of the New York Yankees, sold the club to Dan Topping, Del Webb, and Larry MacPhail for $2,900,000. It was a bargain. The purchase price also gave the trio ownership of the minor league ballparks in Newark, New Jersey, Kansas City, and Binghamton, New York, as well as Yankee Stadium. Larry MacPhail was the driving force behind the deal, and it was MacPhail who would make the key decisions for the club.

MacPhail was a colorful character, a man on the move and a man who liked action. He wasn't afraid of making changes and he was quick to innovate. He also had a genius for making money.

During the winter of 1945–46, he renovated the box seat sections in the Stadium. He was the first to build a bar and a cocktail lounge in a major league ballpark. He installed the best lighting system available at the time for night baseball. It was all intended to bring more money into the club's coffers.

He also developed a spring-training schedule that was sure to swell those coffers, too.

While the general manager with the Cincinnati Reds, he had taken the team to Puerto Rico for spring training. When he was president of the Brooklyn Dodgers, the Bums had trained some in Havana, Cuba.

In 1946, he scheduled the Yankees for spring training in Panama.

It was to Miami, Florida, that Phil Rizzuto, Joe DiMaggio, Bill Dickey, and all the other Yankee ballplayers discharged from Uncle Sam's Armed Forces, reported for spring training. From Miami, they were flown en masse to the city of Balboa in the Panama Canal Zone. MacPhail was making baseball history. This was the first time that a major league club had flown out of the continental United States.

The native population of that little Central American country welcomed the American ballplayers wildly. The men and women who worked for the U.S. government in the Canal were just as excited to see real, live major leaguers playing the game in person. There were crowds of fans at every practice session and intrasquad game, the attendance revenues fattening the Yankee treasury, as MacPhail had predicted. And the Yanks put on a great show for the Panamanian fans, aided and abetted by the always-dynamic Larry MacPhail.

Joe DiMaggio, Charlie Keller, Bill Dickey, and Joe Gordon would take turns swatting the ball out of the park. Joe Gordon and Phil Rizzuto put on almost-unbelievable exhibitions of dexterity in the infield. It was all choreographed by MacPhail —that is, the order of performances was arranged by Mac-Phail—and the play of Gordon and the Scooter around second base came as the climax of each training session.

The coach would slash grounders at the two stars that would have them ranging far and deep for the ball, and, to the cheers of the fans, they would come up with the ball, get it to second, and whoever was there, Phil or Joe, would pivot and whip it to first for the exciting double play.

"Cucaracha" was what they called Phil Rizzuto. Spanish, of course, is the language of Panama, and in Spanish *cucaracha* means "cockroach." (Maybe the fans knew Lefty Gomez—he had called the Scooter a cockroach the very first day Phil reported for duty as a Yankee back in 1941.)

But it wasn't just the Scooter's size that earned him that name in Panama. It was for his agility in the field, his quickness, his fluid motion, that the Spanish-speaking people of Panama dubbed the mighty mite "Cucaracha," lovingly and with a respect that almost amounted to awe. Phil Rizzuto, it would seem, had lost none of his baseball prowess for all the time he had been away from the game in the Navy.

What Phil did lose in the service was ten pounds. His weight was down to 150. He was pale and wan-looking when he came home to Cora. The effects of his bout with malaria had not entirely worn off. But the Panama sun would take care of that pallor on his face. He would develop a healthy tan. The aftereffects of the malaria, however, would continue to take their toll.

Panama seemed to be good for all the Yankees. They all loosened up under the tropical sun. Some of them loosened up a bit too much.

Most of the players in the Yankees' camp had just returned to civilian life. They had been in uniform for as much as three and four years, in some of the fiercest fighting in the Pacific and Europe, or bored to death in some out-of-the-way island post. Free from the stress of battle, the rigid regimentation of the service, or the boredom of military life, they let themselves go in Panama. They played their hardest on the practice field during the daytime. Then they played just as hard at night in the supper clubs, bars, and nightclubs of the Canal Zone.

Not all of them, of course. A lot of the players in their time off just went sight-seeing, shopping, fishing, or to an occasional party thrown by one of the U.S. officials in residence.

Phil Rizzuto was one of the second group, but he even skipped the parties. First, the Scooter doesn't smoke. He doesn't drink hard liquor, either. And he has always liked to go to bed early. Phil was more conscious than most of the importance of good conditioning for an athlete. There was never anything he did, or indulged in, that might have threatened his physical condition.

However, despite his carefulness, the Scooter just couldn't shake that malaria bug. Even after a person is cured of the disease, it can hit him again. And it did.

He had managed to put on some of the weight he had lost in the service. Cora had helped there, feeding him good and nourishing food. But the recurrence of the disease took those pounds off quickly enough.

Joe McCarthy, who missed nothing on the baseball field, was quick to notice this loss of weight. He noticed, too, that Phil wasn't getting to the ball as fast, that there was something missing, that extra sharpness, and that his timing at bat was off as well. When the Scooter began to complain of dizzy spells, a sure sign of malaria, Joe sent him to the government hospital in Ancon, Panama.

The doctors took care of the bug, with sulfa and other antibiotics, and Phil was out of the hospital soon enough. But his weight and his strength came back too slowly. For the most part, Joe McCarthy had the Scooter sitting on the bench for what remained of the games scheduled against various local teams during spring training in Panama. If the shortstop chafed at the bit, eager to get back into the lineup, he didn't say so. Phil knew, as well as anyone else, that he needed the rest the Yankee skipper had imposed on him.

When the Yanks finally packed their bags and returned to the States, they were in great shape. Some said they were in mid-season form. And they showed it by winning every game they played against major league competition in Florida, a string of thirty wins. They were quickly tabbed, by almost every sportswriter, as certain winners of the American League pennant in 1946.

Phil still felt weak at times and would occasionally experience a dizzy spell, but he was sure that he would be in top shape once the regular baseball season started. MacPhail, however, seemed to have a different view of the shortstop situation. Just before an exhibition game with the St. Louis Cardinals in St. Petersburg, the volatile MacPhail set a press conference that was to shock the entire Yankee ballclub, and especially Scooter.

"I want to announce," he said to the assembled sportswriters, his face creased with a big, self-satisfied smile, "that the Yankee organization has acquired Bobby Brown, a shortstop who hit over .400 at Stanford University, the University of California, Los Angeles, and Tulane."

From there he continued to extol the virtues of the twenty-one-year-old Brown.

"Seven other clubs wanted him. Two of them outbid us, but we got him.

"He's the greatest prospect since Honus Wagner played for the Pittsburgh Pirates. New York is lucky to get him."

Sportswriters are pretty down-to-earth guys. They want to see before they believe. And they had heard such talk about "great prospects" before, many times, and about kids who never even came close to making it. They listened to MacPhail all right, but they weren't giving much credence to his words. As a matter of fact, they didn't even bother to conceal the expressions of doubt and even disbelief on their faces.

Larry MacPhail wasn't blind. He knew what those sportswriters were thinking, and he didn't like it. He began a slow burn.

"Mr. MacPhail," someone began.

It was Will Wedge, correspondent for the *New York Sun* (defunct for many years now) and later librarian for the Baseball Hall of Fame in Cooperstown.

Wedge was a veteran newspaperman, white-haired, a distinguished-looking man with a manner to match. He was also blessed with a healthy touch of cynicism, and his satirical sports column could challenge any for its acidity.

"Mr. MacPhail," he asked in his most gentlemanly and casual manner, "is it all right to write that Phil Rizzuto's job will be safe for another two weeks?"

"We don't need any of your sarcasm, Mr. Wedge!" shot back MacPhail, his slow burn becoming a quick boil. He began to storm out of the room.

Cooler heads prevailed and MacPhail returned, but Wedge had made his point.

When Bobby Brown showed up in St. Petersburg the next day, it was obvious that the Scooter had nothing to worry about. Bobby Brown was good, but he wasn't in the same class as Phil Rizzuto.

"Kind of slow," said one newspaperman.

"Doesn't cover too much ground," said another.

"Can't move to the left, can he?"

The Scooter watched young Bobby Brown with mixed emotions. He knew that the kid had been given a $50,000 bonus to sign with the Yankees.

"He's no bargain, is he?" said one of the sportswriters who had come over to Rizzuto to console him. "I think your job is pretty safe."

"Fifty thousand bucks!" said the Scooter. "Holy cow! That's a whole lot more money than they ever paid me. I sure was born too soon."

As for Bobby Brown, he took his turn watching the Scooter play short, and just gaped in wonder at the sheer artistry of the little fellow.

"My goodness," he said. "That guy can certainly play shortstop, can't he?"

One of the sportswriters collared young Brown and asked whether he thought he would be playing the Scooter's spot.

"Not tomorrow," said Brown. "I guess some people must think I'm a pretty good ballplayer. They paid me a heap of money to sign up, and I never played in pro ball before. Yeah, they paid me a lot of money, but I think it will be a long time before I even begin to think of taking Rizzuto's place."

He didn't, ever. When he did enter the Yankee lineup, he was playing at third base. Rizzuto had many good years ahead of him.

1946 started as expected, with the New York Yankees on top of the heap. With Tommy Henrich, Joe DiMaggio, Charlie Keller—the greatest outfielders in the game—back on the team; with Bill Dickey behind the plate again; with Gordon and Rizzuto back in their double-play positions; with Nick

Etten, who led the league in RBIs in 1945 and in homers in 1944, at first base; with George Stirnweiss, the 1945 batting champ, at third; with a pitching staff that boasted such stars as Spud Chandler, Bill Bevens, Red Ruffing, and relief-artist Johnny Murphy, no one could see how the New York club could miss taking the American League pennant, even the World Series.

But miss they did, and 1946 proved a hectic year for the New York Yankees in more ways than one.

Perhaps the team was too cocky, too overconfident, but whatever the cause, the fact is that the Yankees just didn't have it. The Boston Red Sox, on the other hand, the only team that the sportswriters had figured that spring to be any kind of competition for the New York club, just began running away with the race. The Red Sox won forty of their first fifty games for an amazing winning percentage of .800. The rest of the league, including the Yankees, seemed to be conceding the American League championship to the Bean Town club.

This didn't sit too well with the ambitious Larry MacPhail. There were heated words between MacPhail and the skipper of the Yanks, Joe McCarthy. The fat was in the fire. Before the end of May 1946, Joe McCarthy, after a most brilliant career with the New York Yankees, resigned.

"It is with extreme regret that you must accept my resignation," was the odd message McCarthy wired to MacPhail.

"As you know," MacPhail responded, "I have been extremely reluctant to accept your resignation."

But MacPhail did accept the resignation, and McCarthy, who had won eight league pennants and seven world championships for the New York club, was out.

Bill Dickey, who at the age of thirty-nine was playing his seventeenth year as catcher for the Yankees, was given the job of trying to get the team out of the doldrums. Yankee fans acknowledged Joe McCarthy's ability, but the appointment of Dickey as manager met with little opposition. Dickey had long been a hero among the Bronx rooters. They pulled for him wholeheartedly to get the Yankees moving again. When Dickey took over as manager, the Yankees were five games behind the Red Sox.

But the task was somewhat beyond even big Bill. The Yanks, with the possible exception of Charlie Keller, who hit thirty home runs, did not hit well at all. 1946 was the year Joe DiMaggio, for the first time in his career, failed to hit .300, finishing the season at .290. Rizzuto, far below his prewar form, hit .257. Gordon was plagued with injuries and hit a minuscule .210. Not one Yankee regular hit .300 in 1946. Except for Chandler, Bevans, and Randy Gumpert, the pitching was not up to Yankee standards. And there was dissension on the team. Things got so bad in the clubhouse that Joe Gordon had to call a press conference to deny there was any friction between him and his once inseparable pal, Bill Dickey.

None of this helped the Scooter, always sensitive to any kind of disharmony. The bickering, bad press, the failure of the Yankees troubled him. His batting average on July 17 was a puny .222, not even up to the poor team average of .239. Perhaps if he hadn't been hampered by bruised and knotted muscles in his thighs, and by those dizzy spells that just wouldn't go away, he might have avoided an accident that almost killed him.

In a game against St. Louis in July, a fast ball thrown by Nelson Potter, the Browns' right-hander, hit the Scooter in the left temple. He went down like a man shot, and a stretcher crew carried him off the field.

His mother was watching the game, and even before the

horrified gasp in the stands had died down, she was in the dressing room, praying, as ice packs were applied to her son's head.

An ambulance arrived hurriedly and rushed Phil off to New York Hospital for observation. They took X rays of his skull. Happily, the X rays showed there had been no fracture. The ball had hit him squarely, but not too high on his temple. A little higher, where the wall of flesh is somewhat weaker, and there might very well have been serious brain damage. The Scooter had taken the impact of that fast ball mostly on the upper portion of his cheekbone. Phil was certainly groggy but he had never lost consciousness.

"I can't understand why I couldn't get away from that pitch," wondered the Scooter.

"The ball sailed," his pals told him. "You were lucky. It might have been much worse."

"Yeah," said the Scooter. "Lucky it wasn't Feller pitching."

Bob Feller was a great fast-ball pitcher for the Cleveland Indians. He was going to set a record of 348 strikeouts in 1946 and had already pitched a no-hitter that year against the New York Yankees. Phil *was* lucky that Feller hadn't thrown the ball that sent him to the hospital.

The hospital sent him home only two days after he had been carried in on a stretcher, but painful headaches and dizzy spells put him back in the hospital again.

Again the hospital kept him for only two days and sent him home, and inside of a week he was back in the Yankee lineup. Some of his teammates wondered what that beaning would do to the Scooter. Good hitters like Joe Medwick of the Brooklyn Dodgers and Hank Leiber of the New York Giants became gun-shy after they had been beaned at the peaks of their careers and were never the sluggers they had been after returning to the game. But Scooter's teammates didn't have to be concerned. The enforced rest had helped him regain his strength, and he didn't show the slightest evidence of fear when he got a bat in his hand. In fact, playing as if the Yanks still had a chance for the pennant, the Scooter gave the game every ounce of his vigor and spirit.

But it wasn't a very good year for the New York club, which wound up the season in third place, seventeen games behind the rampaging Red Sox. Dickey was fired as the season drew to a close and coach Johnny Neun was appointed the manager for the remainder of 1946. Johnny Neun wouldn't last long, either.

The only exciting aspect of the 1946 season for the Yankees, and a few other major league players, was the emergence of the Pasquel brothers, Jorge and Bernardo, and their bizarre effort to lure some of the best in both major leagues down to Mexico for a "Great Mexican Baseball League."

10

The Great
Mexican League Mess

Jorge and Bernardo Pasquel were two of the richest men south of the Rio Grande. They had built their great fortune in the import business, among others. They looked to baseball, next to bullfighting Mexico's most popular sport, to add to the multimillions they had already accumulated in a number of banks.

They were a couple of hard businessmen, but they were not without a romantic flair. Jorge walked around with two pearl-and-diamond-studded revolvers in side holsters. He said they were for protection but, at the drop of a hat, was quick to tell his audience, any audience, how he had once killed a man.

"In self-defense, of course," he would add, though his listeners might doubt it.

Importers by trade, they had hit upon the idea of importing the best in American baseball to Mexico. It seemed all very logical to them. They had been successful importing everything else, so why not import men, particularly baseball men? Not only would the importing of baseball players prove profitable, they figured, adding to their already uncountable millions, but it would make them superheroes in their native land, raising the quality of the game in their country to major league levels. They could see a World Series that included Mexican ballclubs. They even began to imagine that their popularity in Mexico would become so great, because of their baseball coup, that the people might very well elect them to the presidency of their republic.

And how would they import the American ballplayers? The same way they imported everything else. With money. They believed that everything and everybody had its price, and they were willing to pay it.

The Pasquels quietly set their plan in motion in the winter of 1945 and the spring of 1946. It's rare when a businessman shows all his cards at the beginning of a deal. The Mexican brothers knew that their raids on the American big leagues would have to start small, that they couldn't go after the biggest guns in the majors right off. More than anyone else playing the game, they wanted Joe DiMaggio. Everyone in Mexico, as well as the United States, knew Joe DiMaggio. He would have been a great drawing card anywhere in the world, and especially south of the border. But they knew it wasn't good strategy to go after Joe first; they went after the stars, all right, but those a notch or two below the great DiMaggio.

They went after George Stirnweiss and Phil Rizzuto in Panama, where the Yanks were in spring training in 1946. Like the sharp businessmen they were, there was nothing concrete in their offer to the ballplayers, but they intimated there was a good deal waiting for the two Yankees if they walked out of the New York organization.

Neither Phil nor Stirnweiss said no to the proposition, but they didn't say yes, either. George Stirnweiss, who had been the American League batting champion in 1945, was dreaming of a great future in Yankee pinstripes. The Scooter, who had some doubts about his ability to return to his prewar baseball form, was a bit more interested. The one thing that did bother the Scooter about the offer was his bout with malaria. The thought of playing baseball in tropical Mexico troubled him. In any case, for a while anyway, as he continued to fight his poor health in Panama, he forgot about the Pasquel brothers and their Mexican League.

The Pasquels, in turn, forgot about George Stirnweiss, as the young ballplayer got off to a poor start in the regulation 1946 baseball season. But they didn't forget the Scooter.

One day, early in the season, as Phil was leaving Yankee Stadium and walking to his car, he was stopped by a fellow he hardly remembered.

"We spoke in Panama," said the stranger, and it all came back to the Scooter. This was the man who had come to him with the Pasquels' proposition.

"Do you want to see Mr. Pasquel? He's here." The stranger pointed. "In that car."

Phil hesitated for a moment, looked the stranger over, decided he had nothing to lose.

There were three men in the car and Phil didn't know any of them.

"This is Mr. Pasquel," said the stranger.

"Let's get out of here fast," Phil responded worriedly. "What if MacPhail sees us!"

Two things were uppermost in Phil's mind at the moment. One, he didn't want to incur the wrath of Larry MacPhail, who might fire him for having even the slightest contact with the Mexicans. Two, there was the decree of Happy Chandler, commissioner of baseball at the time, that anyone who jumped to the Mexican League would be banned from major league ball for five years.

The Pasquels had had some success in luring big leaguers down to Mexico. Their biggest coup, up to that moment, was Mickey Owen, the Dodger catcher who had dropped that third strike in the Dodgers' loss to the Yankees in the 1941 World Series.

The five men in the car drove to the West Side Highway and parked underneath the roadway. It was a dark and spooky area. Bernardo and Phil got out of the automobile and walked behind one of the pillars supporting the overhead structure. Before one word was spoken, Bernardo reached into his pocket and pulled out a fat, fat roll of bills.

"They were all thousand dollar bills," the Scooter was to report later. "At least, they were all thousand dollar bills on top of that wad."

"Here," said Bernardo Pasquel unceremoniously. "Take this money. It's for you. For nothing. Come to Mexico. Leave right away with my chauffeur. Your family. Everything. We fix."

Phil didn't take the money. Instinctively, he knew it would be a mistake.

They returned to the car.

Pasquel offered Phil a bonus of $10,000 on signing and an additional $15,000 for the season.

Fifteen thousand was twice as much as the Yankees were paying him for that year, but Phil still hesitated.

"We'll give you a five-year contract. Twelve thousand a year. And the $10,000 bonus."

The Scooter's head was swimming in numbers but something told him that it wouldn't be right to shake hands on the proposition just yet.

"Let me think about it," he said. "I want to talk it over with my wife."

When Phil got home, after thinking all the way about all that money he could make playing in the Mexican League, he was so excited that he gave Cora an even bigger hug and kiss than usual.

"What is it?" asked Cora. She knew her husband well enough to know that something special had happened. "Did you go four for four?"

"Better than that," said Phil.

"Five for five?" asked Cora, raising her eyebrows in surprise.

"Better still," answered Phil, beaming from ear to ear. "I'm going to make a hundred thousand dollars!"

"How? How?" screamed Cora, as excited as Phil now. "Tell me how!"

Phil told her the story, and, as it unfolded, Cora became less and less enthusiastic. She certainly didn't like the idea of him meeting under an elevated highway in the dark to make a deal.

"Why all the cloak-and-dagger stuff?" she questioned.

"Pasquel is afraid that the Yanks will take him to court, try to stop him," Phil tried to explain.

"Let's think about it," advised Cora.

"I don't know," said Phil. "I'm not working for Barrow anymore. You can't tell anything about Larry MacPhail, and there's a lot of talk about Joe McCarthy quitting or being fired. This deal with Pasquel is a lot of money. Security. We could do a lot of things with all that money."

"Let's wait," cautioned Cora. "Let's think about it."

Somehow the newspapers learned of Pasquel's effort to sign

up Phil. The New York Yankees' front office got wind of the story, too. The next afternoon, Cora had two visitors. The first was a Newark newspaperman.

"No," Cora told the newspaperman, "Phil hasn't signed any contract with the Pasquel brothers."

The second visitor was George Weiss, chief of the Yankee farm system. He came as an emissary for Larry MacPhail. George looked worried.

"No," repeated Cora. "Phil hasn't signed."

George Weiss looked relieved, for a moment.

"Not yet," she added.

"Not yet?" repeated Weiss, grim-faced again.

"Do you want to keep Phil?" asked Cora.

Weiss didn't answer.

"Then give him a raise."

Cora knew that George Weiss couldn't give Phil that raise, but she knew he would carry the message home to Larry MacPhail.

That very same evening, both Cora and Phil were invited to the Pasquel headquarters in the Waldorf-Astoria, one of New York's poshest hotels. They met in the Wedgewood Room. There were the Pasquel brothers, Jorge and Bernardo, their lawyers, and a number of glamor girls, Mexican and American. Dinner was served on gold plates, and there was, of course, champagne.

"They had orchids for Cora," said Phil, "and Pasquel wore a diamond ring the size of an egg. He caught me staring at it and wanted to give it to me. I had a hard time shaking my head."

And there was talk.

One of the women spent the whole evening extolling the

virtues of Mexico to Cora. Bernardo got Mickey Owen on the phone, in Mexico, and had the telephone brought to the table so that Phil could talk to him.

"Owen told me how wonderful everything was down there," said the Scooter. "He made it sound like the greatest deal in the world. I was impressed, but I keep thinking now that he maybe had a gun at his back!"

Nevertheless, Phil was impressed. He was even more impressed as the Pasquels kept raising the ante. It got so that he was offered a $15,000 bonus, a salary of $20,000, a Cadillac, an air-conditioned apartment in Mexico City, and three servants.

It was an offer that was almost impossible to refuse.

But the Pasquels made two mistakes that night. First, they kept knocking the Yankees. That didn't sit too well with Phil, who felt a great deal of loyalty to the team and all the fellows he had played with.

Second, Bernardo Pasquel, boasting of his brother's toughness, told the story of how Jorge had killed a man, dramatically embellishing his tale with all the appropriate gestures. This was too much for Cora.

"Let's go home, Phil," she said.

They left, Phil with Pasquel's top offer written on a menu. He still has that menu.

"It's a souvenir of a mistake we almost made," he says.

Cora liked the financial end of the deal, but nothing else. She particularly didn't like the idea of living in a country where men went around with pearl-handled guns, killed people, then bragged about it.

Of course the picture she got was not the real Mexico, but she didn't know any other.

Phil's mother added her voice to the opposition, too.

"You'll be like a man without a country. How can you bring up the children that way? It would be a disgrace."

Phil and Cora had only one child at the time, Patti, but the Scooter's mother's message was clear.

Still, says Phil, "I admit that I was ready to go, right then and there. I was really afraid that this was my last year with the Yankees, anyway."

They were still batting the proposition around in the Rizzuto home when George Weiss paid his second visit. This time he had his wife along, maybe for support, maybe to help him win over Cora.

George came right to the point.

"Joe McCarthy sent me over. He said he had heard you're on your way to Mexico. I want to talk to you about it."

Phil was willing to listen, but, before George Weiss could get too far, the phone rang. Joe McCarthy was calling.

More talk. More advice. More warning.

The Scooter was just about fed up. The more hassle he got, the more he leaned toward jumping the Yankees in favor of Mexico.

"Do me one favor," said George Weiss before he left the Rizzutos. "Don't leave until you see MacPhail."

Phil promised, but his mind was just about set.

In the morning, he walked into the office of the president of the Yankees, Larry MacPhail.

MacPhail was in a wild mood, and he let Phil have it for even listening to the Pasquels.

For once Phil didn't care what MacPhail said, or did. For once Phil was in the driver's seat, and he knew it.

"OK, Mr. MacPhail," he said, after the club president was

through blustering, "I'll stay if you'll give me a $10,000 bonus."

MacPhail went red in the face. He bounced out of his chair. He raged and he raved.

"Bonus!" he bellowed. "I want you to sit down and sign a complaint against the Pasquels."

That way, he would have the evidence needed to go to court and get an injunction to stop the Mexicans from dealing with his ballplayers.

But Phil wasn't signing anything.

"Why should I?" he asked. "They're only trying to help me. All they want to do is give me more money to play ball. If you want to," he said boldly, "you can do the same thing!"

Larry wasn't beaten yet.

"If you don't sign that complaint, I'll suspend you!" he threatened.

The Scooter almost smiled at him.

"Suspension won't mean anything, will it," he said, "if I go to Mexico."

MacPhail was licked.

He fumed and fretted for a while, then offered the Scooter a $5,000 bonus to stick with the Yankees.

"Ten thousand," said Phil.

"Five thousand now," countered MacPhail. "Five thousand more if you have a good season."

It was a deal.

It was really Cora's victory. She was the one who had suggested the bonus in the first place.

Larry MacPhail did institute injunction proceedings against the Pasquels, but Phil's name was not among the list of plaintiffs.

As for that second $5,000, Phil didn't have that good a year. He forgot about the $5,000, and Larry MacPhail never mentioned it.

And as for the Pasquels' dream of a great Mexican League and national glory, it fizzled quickly and turned into a nightmare for the eighteen major leaguers who defected: they were barred from playing ball in the U.S. until June 1949, when the commissioner's original five-year ban was lifted.

11

World Champs Again

Bucky Harris was signed by Larry MacPhail to manage the Yankees in 1947. Harris was the "boy wonder" who had piloted the Washington Senators to successive pennants in 1924 and 1925 when he was not yet thirty years old. Bucky was an independent character. He would take no guff from the front office. He was also a very private person. When his day's work at the ballpark was over, so were his dealings with his ballplayers—his personal life was his own affair. He even had an unlisted telephone number—a number he wouldn't give anybody, not even the top brass in the Yankee organization. This didn't sit well with MacPhail or George Weiss, who called him a "four-hour manager." Eventually it would lead to considerable difficulty, but Larry MacPhail bet on him for 1947, and the bet paid off.

There were other changes that year. Frank Crosetti signed as a player-coach, though he would be coaching more than he would be playing. Joe DiMaggio went into the hospital to have a bone spur removed from his left heel in January of that year, and it wasn't to be his last trip to the hospital. Joe Gordon was traded to the Cleveland Indians for Allie Reynolds, who would prove to be a great addition to the Yanks, winning 131 games in the eight seasons he pitched for the club. George (Snuffy) Stirnweiss, who had mostly played third base in 1946, was shifted to second, where he and the Scooter would develop into a smooth double-play combination in short order.

George McQuinn, who had been Yankee property back in 1932 and then had played with the Athletics and the Browns, was picked up as a free agent by the Yankees. He played first base and did as much and more than was expected of him. He would hit .304, including thirteen home runs, and he made only eight errors during the 1947 season for a fielding percentage of .994.

Billy (the Bull) Johnson would play third base. He was kind of slow on his feet, but he had a great pair of hands and was a top infielder.

Larry (Yogi) Berra, who was to write his name indelibly in the annals of baseball, was a newcomer. The Yanks had turned down an offer of $50,000 by the New York Giants for Yogi, who had played for the Yankees' Kansas City farm club in 1946. He was to become one of the greatest catchers in the history of the game.

There were others new to a Yankee uniform in 1947, notably pitcher Frank (Spec) Shea, who won fourteen games for the New York club that year. And Joe Page came in from the bullpen to emerge as the greatest fire-balling reliever in the league.

Spring training for the Yankees in 1947 started February 15. On that day, Bucky Harris led his Yankees from New York to San Juan, Puerto Rico. There were to be other stops outside of mainland USA. MacPhail, in his usual quest for the dollar, had arranged the tour. After San Juan there was

Caracas, Venezuela, and Havana, Cuba, before the troops could settle down to business in St. Petersburg, Florida.

But Bucky Harris, who didn't think much of shuttling around in planes and playing on foreign soil, was smart enough to avoid the errors of spring training the year before in Panama. He wasn't going to let his players wear themselves out, playing ball in the hot tropical sun during the day and carousing in the night spots until the wee hours of the morning. Bucky wisely let the older players work out their own training program, and he didn't press them too hard or work them too long in the hot sun. He wanted a strong, well-conditioned, and fresh team, ready and willing for the long season ahead.

Bucky Harris skillfully maneuvered his ballplayers through spring training. The Yanks weren't going to fold, from what Bucky felt was over-confidence and poor performance, as they had in 1946, not if he could help it.

The Bucky Harris treatment was exactly what Phil Rizzuto needed after that miserable 1946 season. He kept his optimum playing weight. There weren't any of those dizzy spells. He played in all but one of the scheduled 154 games, and he fielded his position as brilliantly as ever.

When Harris, his coaches, and the writers who traveled with the club gathered for a few drinks after each victory, there'd be a toast to Joe DiMaggio, to Joe Page, to Tommy Henrich, to any of the players who had contributed to the win.

"And don't forget little Phil!"

That was Bucky Harris. He wasn't forgetting "little Phil" and he didn't want anyone else to forget him, either.

"He pulls a miracle out there every day," said the skipper. "I wouldn't trade him for any shortstop in baseball. I don't care if he hits only .250, it's what he does with his glove, the way he saves our pitchers, that makes him great. I don't believe I've ever seen a game where he didn't make at least one great play."

Phil did better than .250 in 1947. He hit for a .273 average. Of his one hundred fifty hits that year, he had twenty-six doubles, nine triples, and two home runs.

John (Red) Corriden, one of Bucky Harris's lieutenants, was even more enthusiastic in his praise of the mighty mite. Lollypop Corriden, as the ballplayers called him, had been around for a long time. It was Corriden who was largely responsible for the development of that other great shortstop, Peewee Reese, when Corriden was with the Dodgers. He had a lot of sweet words for Peewee, but nothing like those he had for the Scooter.

"I've been in baseball for more than forty years," he said, "and I'll be darned if I ever knew a ballplayer with the priceless, perfect disposition of Rizzuto.

"Phil's a sweetheart. He means a tremendous lot to the team because everyone likes him and responds to his cheery manner and is the better for it.

"Phil, you might say, is the sparkplug of the Yankees. He's the balance wheel that keeps the team spinning along merrily and successfully. His value can't be measured by mere fielding and batting averages. It's something that goes deeper. Growls and gripes in the locker room after a bad day disappear quickly with Rizzuto around. No team can get into the dumps with Phil to pep things up.

"I know Reese and admire him. But I have to go for Phil because of his disposition and the cute way he has of binding the Yankee infield into a perfect unit."

That was quite a speech Lollypop Corriden made. It helps us understand better all those tricks his teammates played on the Scooter and the way he took them.

There wasn't a Yankee who didn't know that the Scooter was deathly afraid of snakes, mice, and other little creatures, and there wasn't a Yankee who didn't use this knowledge for a bit of sport. In the clubhouse, in the locker room, out in the field, the Scooter was never safe from the pranks they played on him. There'd be a snake, or something that looked like one, suddenly slithering down his face as he laced his shoes in the dressing room. There'd be the shout, "Look out, Phil!" as some small, furry object that might have been a dead mouse came hurtling through space at him. There were bugs, worms, eels, even an occasional frog, which they'd put in his baseball glove, just to hear the cry of fear and surprise he'd let out as his fingers came into contact with the slimy thing. It got so that all they had to do was approach Phil with their hands closed over some imaginary thing to scare the Scooter out of his wits.

They loved him. Sometimes they showed their affection in funny ways; other times their displays were much more dramatic.

For instance, in a game against the Red Sox in 1946, Johnny Pesky came barreling into second base when the Scooter was covering the bag. Pesky hit Phil with his shoulder and knocked him cold. The Yanks charged; the Red Sox responded. There were some punches thrown and some shoving but no battle royal—the Yankees just wanted the Sox to know how they felt about anyone getting rough with their precious shortstop.

Then there was the time, in 1947, in a game against Detroit, when pitcher Art Houtteman hit the Scooter with an inside fastball. The Yanks immediately went to work on him, though not with their fists. Nine men batted around, and Houtteman, who had had the game safely won before he hit Rizzuto, found himself suddenly in the showers.

That incident had a repeat performance. Again that year Houtteman had his game won. Again he hit Phil with a pitch. And again the Yanks batted around, sending Houtteman to the showers.

"Pitchers ought to know better," said sportswriter Garry Schumacher. "When you hit that little Rizzuto, it's like hitting a cop."

Once after a brawl that was started when an opposing baserunner plowed into Rizzuto and left him in a heap, Red Ruffing, the great Yankee hurler, said, "You know, if that little guy had been hurt, I think I would have cried." Such were the testimonials of the Yankees' love.

In the 1947 season Phil wasn't the only one who returned to prewar form. Tommy Henrich, Johnny Lindell, Charlie Keller, and Joe DiMaggio hit the ball solidly, and DiMaggio, despite the time spent in hospitals, emerged the winner of the American League's Most Valuable Player award. Stirnweiss made the fans forget the absence of Joe Gordon, and Billy Johnson was outstanding at third base, while the veteran McQuinn, at first base, was second only to DiMaggio in batting average.

Allie Reynolds won nineteen games in his first year as a Yankee, Spec Shea won fourteen, and so did Joe Page. In July the Yankees strengthened their pitching corps with the addition of Vic Raschi and Louis (Bobo) Newsom. Raschi was brought up from Portland in the Pacific Coast League. The

Yanks got Newsom on waivers from the Washington Senators. "Have no fear, Bobo's here," announced the veteran hurler. He sang it out. It was his favorite song.

"You're in, boys," he declared enthusiastically. "With Bobo on your side, you can't miss!"

Well, Bobo contributed seven wins to the Yankees' cause, and the rookie Raschi seven more. By September 5, the New York club had won itself another pennant and was headed for another World Series against their rivals across the river, the Brooklyn Dodgers.

The Dodgers, managed by Burt Shotton, had a roster of players whose names will long be remembered. There were Eddie Stanky, Peewee Reese, Pete Reiser, Carl Furillo, and Dixie Walker, the "People's Choice," among others. And, above all, they had the great Jackie Robinson, the first black man to play in the major leagues, and one of the most exciting players in the history of organized baseball. But curiously enough, it was a couple of other Dodgers, the veteran Cookie Lavagetto and the almost unknown Al Gionfriddo, who were responsible for the most dramatic moments in that World Series.

The Yankees started the Series in high gear. They took the first game, 5–3. A fifth inning five-run rally was all the Yanks needed, as Joe Page came in to mop up the game for Frank Shea.

In the second game, with Allie Reynolds pitching, the Yanks blasted Dodger hurling for fifteen hits and ran away with a 10–3 victory.

But the Dodgers weren't through. In the third game they jumped all over Bobo Newsom and Vic Raschi in the second inning, scoring six runs. The Yankees came back to score in the third inning on Rizzuto's single, Bill Johnson's double, and

George McQuinn's two-RBI single. The Dodgers answered with a run in the bottom of the inning. In the fourth both teams came up with two more runs each. A homer by Joe DiMaggio with John Lindell aboard accounted for a pair of runs in the Yankee fifth. Then Yogi Berra pinch-hit in the sixth inning and homered—the first pinch-hit home run ever hit in a World Series. Billy Johnson had a grand chance in that same inning to send the Yanks ahead, but he popped up for an easy out with the bases full. In the seventh frame, the Yanks pushed across one more tally. In the eighth inning, Rizzuto worked Hugh Casey, the Dodgers' great relief pitcher, to a 3 and 2 count and then calmly slapped a single to center. Tommy Henrich walked, Lindell got an infield hit, and the bases were full. Then to the great delight and relief of some 33,000 Dodger rooters, Casey carefully pitched to Joe DiMaggio and ended the threat by getting Joe to hit into a double play. The Dodgers had clinched the seesaw game, 9–8.

It was the fourth game of the fall classic that produced the most dramatic moments in the clash between the two clubs.

Bucky Harris pulled a surprise by sending Bill Bevens to the mound. Bevens had won only seven while losing thirteen during the regular season. But Bill Bevens was to surprise everybody in the ballpark that afternoon. He was wild, walked ten men in the game, but the Dodgers were held hitless for eight full innings. When the Dodgers did manage to hit the ball solidly, there was always Tommy Henrich, Johnny Lindell, or Joe DiMaggio to glove it. The Dodgers had managed to fashion one run on a couple of walks, a sacrifice, and an infield out, but the Yanks had scored twice, once on a walk that forced in a run, the second on a triple off the bat of Bill Johnson and a double by Johnny Lindell.

In the bottom of the ninth, the first Dodger to bat went

down quietly. Then Bruce Edwards sent a long fly to Tommy Henrich. Two away. One more and Bevens would have an unbelievable World Series no-hitter—the first in history.

But Carl Furillo drew a walk, the ninth Dodger to get a free pass to first base. Shotton sent Al Gionfriddo in to run for Furillo, and Gionfriddo, to everyone's surprise, took off for second and stole it. Reiser, up next, was a dangerous hitter, and he was intentionally walked.

There were two men on base now, and still two out.

Cookie Lavagetto came in to bat for Eddie Stanky.

Cookie was playing his last year in the major leagues. He had hit only .261 during the season. He didn't seem like much of a threat the way Bill Bevens was pitching.

Bevens's first pitch to Lavagetto was a strike. Bevens seemed to be in control. His next pitch, however, was high, and Cookie got hold of it and sent it screaming to right field, where it hit high on the concrete wall. The Brooklyn fans went wild as two Dodgers came around the bases to score two runs. All at once Bevens had been robbed of a no-hitter, the Yankees were losers, 3–2, and the World Series was evened at two apiece.

The Yankees took the Series lead once again, beating the Dodgers 2–1, in the fifth game. The Dodgers came back to win the next game, 8–6, to knot the Series again. It was in this sixth game that little Al Gionfriddo made the "impossible" catch of a line drive headed for the bullpen in left field, robbing Joe DiMaggio of a certain home run that would have tied the ballgame.

That was the last win for the Dodgers, however, in the 1947 World Series. In the seventh and deciding game, Joe Page came into the game in the fifth inning and allowed the Dodgers just one hit the rest of the way, successfully protecting a 5–2 lead. Page gave up that hit to Eddie Miksis with one out in the ninth, then Bruce Edwards drove a hot one into the Scooter's territory; the Scooter raced into the hole, scooped up the ball, tossed it to Stirnweiss at second, and Stirnweiss fired it to first base. Double play and the Series was over. Once more the Yankees were world champions.

That double play was to be remembered for some time, at least in the Yankee locker room.

"Who's the unhappiest man in baseball?" yelled Lollypop Corriden, day in and day out.

"Bruce Edwards!" came the reply in unison.

"And why is he the unhappiest man in baseball?" Corriden would continue.

"Because the damned fool hit the ball to Rizzuto!"

Of course the Scooter loved it.

He had had a good season. He had had an outstanding World Series, making impossible plays at shortstop while fielding 1.000 and getting eight hits, stealing two bases, and batting .308.

It was a great year for Phil for another reason. On April 19, 1947, Cora had given birth to their second child, Cynthia Ann.

1947 was indeed a marvelous year for Phil Rizzuto. 1948 would be less kind.

12

You Gotta Have Heart

1948 was a frustrating year for the New York Yankees and some of its players, particularly Phil Rizzuto.

MacPhail was gone. He had departed right after the 1947 World Series. George Weiss became general manager of the club, and Weiss and the skipper, Bucky Harris, never had seen eye to eye on how to run a ballclub. Weiss was especially upset over Harris's insistence on keeping his private life private. It was Weiss who had called Bucky the "four-hour manager."

But that wasn't the worst of it. Spud Chandler and Bill Bevens developed sore arms, and the 1947 season was their last in the big leagues. Joe Page, who had been great in relief in 1947, lost much of his effectiveness and wound up with a 7–8 record. Spec Shea, Yankee Rookie of the Year in 1947, was a disaster on the mound for half the season. He had put on too much weight during the winter, and he, too, developed arm trouble. Red Embree, who had been obtained from the Cleveland Indians, didn't fulfill his promise and was only half the pitcher the Yanks had expected.

Still, the Yankees were in the race for the pennant all the way and were eliminated by the Red Sox from the race just two days before the end of the season. And they had to win most of the games without their "sparkplug," the Scooter.

In the very first week of the pennant race, Phil tore a muscle in his right thigh. It was a deep-seated muscle tear that hemorrhaged and kept him out of the lineup. The Scooter had to sit the injury out on the bench three times in the first month of the season.

There was nothing he could do about the injury but wait, rest, and let nature take its course. There was no other remedy.

Phil had to remember the leg ailment he had had in Norfolk, the gangrene that had almost cost him his leg and his baseball career. It didn't make him feel too good. Looking down at that thigh, all black and blue, he couldn't help feeling, as he had felt in 1946 on his return from the service, that maybe he was on the way out, finished as a ballplayer.

The Scooter did get into a game once in a while, but only with his leg tightly taped to give it support and kill the pain. The pain never did leave him throughout the 1948 season.

He missed thirteen games in May. Bobby Brown, who replaced him at shortstop, was hitting the ball at a .381 clip, but Bucky Harris yanked Brown and put the Scooter back in the lineup at the end of May.

Bucky knew that Phil and only Phil could make the great plays at short. He was the key to the infield, and an inspiration.

"I played on one leg," recalled Phil.

One leg seemed plenty for the Yankee skipper, but in June Phil was hit by another ailment. The dizzy spells began to plague him again. All he had to do was look up to catch a pop fly in the sun and his head would start spinning. To make things worse, he was bothered by the heat, which had never affected him before. His eyes seemed to go out of focus. The Scooter certainly had his miseries.

When the Yanks left New York on a western road trip, Bucky Harris had Phil stay behind to consult a physician about his condition.

"Maybe you need eyeglasses," suggested Bucky.

"Maybe," said Phil, but he was afraid something worse was afflicting him, something that couldn't be cured.

Once again, the Scooter felt that his days on the diamond were numbered.

But the doctor was more optimistic.

"You don't need glasses," he said. "I'm sure we can clear up your trouble with some eye exercises.

"Eye exercises?" asked Phil incredulously. He had heard of all kinds of exercises, but eye exercises?

Nevertheless, he followed the doctor's orders, did the exercises, and both the dizzy spells and the failures in focus disappeared.

Fine! But the very next month, July, the Scooter developed arm trouble. He had experienced some elbow stiffness before, in spring training, but the stiffness had always disappeared after a short while. This was something else.

Some people labeled the Scooter a hypochondriac. He certainly spent a great deal of time worrying about his health. But he wasn't dreaming up this arm ailment.

X rays showed there were bone chips in his throwing arm. An operation was in order, but Phil dreaded even the thought of surgery. He played on, but it was obvious to everybody— fans, writers, and the opposition—that his throwing arm didn't have the old snap, speed, or accuracy. The reason was quite simple: it hurt every time he threw. The long throw from deep short to first base was particularly painful, and anyone who was witness could see the pain etched on his face.

When the season was over, the Scooter, along with Joe Di-Maggio, who was suffering the same ailment, went down to Johns Hopkins Hospital in Baltimore to see Dr. George E. Bennett, a surgeon well-known among athletes of every sport.

The doctor told DiMaggio he needed surgery.

As for the Scooter, the doctor, perhaps seeing how worried Phil was, was of the opinion that a delay in surgery wouldn't hurt.

"It may clear up on its own. I think you have to rest the arm. No throwing at all," said Dr. Bennett, and the Scooter skipped out of the hospital as happy as a kid with a new bicycle.

Fortunately for the Scooter, the condition did clear up. That and the Phil Rizzuto Day at Yankee Stadium he had been given on August 29 were perhaps the only high points in the year for him.

There were the presents, of course, on Phil Rizzuto Day—a television set, a yellow Olds convertible, and other goodies—but, for all the joy he derived from the fans' shower of appreciation, Phil was troubled.

As at the end of 1946, when the Scooter was sure that his career was just about over, so he went home after his "Day" at the Stadium in 1948.

He hadn't given much thought to what he would do after he had retired from baseball. Now he began to think about it. He had a wife and two children to support and no trade, no profession he could fall back on. Baseball had always been his life. It had to continue, one way or another, to be his way of making a living.

Actually, the Scooter had no real reason to worry, not just then. For just around the corner was the finest year in his career.

At the end of the 1948 season, George Weiss fired manager Bucky Harris. In the middle of October he signed Casey Stengel to manage the Yanks. Charles Dillon Stengel, who, legend has it, had given up the study of dentistry because he was left-handed and left-handed dental tools were hard to come by, had been one of the more colorful players in the major leagues for fourteen years. In the twilight of his career, playing for the New York Giants, he had banged out two home runs, beating the Yankees in two games of the 1923 World Series. His batting average for three World Series was an amazing .393.

He was known, too, for some of the zaniest antics ever pulled on the field and off. Once while playing for the Pirates, he doffed his baseball hat to a jeering crowd at Ebbets Field in Brooklyn, and a tiny sparrow flew out of it. The zaniest gag of all was "the great grapefruit caper" pulled on Dodger manager Wilbert Robinson.

Ruth Law, an attractive young aviatrix, was flying her plane over Daytona Beach, Florida, in the spring of 1916, and as a publicity stunt she and a sporting goods agent dropped some golf balls from a height of 1,000 feet. Among those who watched the demonstration were a group of Dodgers, who were there for spring training.

"I bet I could catch a baseball thrown out of that plane," said Uncle Robbie, a former catcher for various major league clubs.

The players argued the point.

"Not from that height," Robbie admitted. "But from about four hundred feet I could do it."

Miss Law agreed to the stunt, and the next day there was a big crowd to see Robbie grapple with the law of gravity.

Frank Kelly, the Dodgers' trainer, volunteered to go up in the plane and drop the ball.

When Kelly climbed into the plane, he carried not a baseball, but a large grapefruit that Stengel had given him to drop instead.

Robbie set himself for the catch as the plane came down, and when it leveled off at about 400 feet, he saw what looked like a ball come flying down at him. Then, as he tried to clutch the missile, it whistled right through his hands, struck him on the chest, and burst, knocking him down and drenching his face and body with citrus juice.

"Oh, God! I'm killed! I'm blind! It's broke open my chest. I'm covered with blood! Somebody help me!"

When Robbie heard the roar of laughter, he slowly opened his eyes, saw he wasn't bleeding, and got up quickly.

"You . . . wise guys," he yelled. "You . . . clowns!"

A little while later, after he had changed his shirt, he burst into laughter at the wildest stunt ever pulled in baseball circles.

He instinctively knew that it was a Stengel trick, and from that day on, whenever he looked at Casey, it was with menace.

Though Casey was a great prankster, he hadn't been very successful as a big league manager up to this point. He had managed the Brooklyn Dodgers from 1934–36 and the Boston Braves from 1938–43 and had gotten nowhere with them. But then again, they were teams nobody could have done anything with.

But in 1948 he had piloted the Oakland Acorns to the championship of the Pacific Coast League and had developed some fine young players, among them Billy Martin and Jackie

Jensen. The Yankees felt they could take a chance on him, and it was a chance that was going to pay off for a number of years to come. Right from the start with the New York club, Casey showed the baseball world that he was a lot more than a clown. It was to learn that few people knew baseball as well as Old Case.

And Casey certainly knew the value of Phil Rizzuto, both as a ballplayer and as an asset to a team.

"He can do anything anybody else ever did with a baseball," he said of the Scooter. "He does a lot of things better. How about how he goes for a hopper over the pitcher's head? He's the best I've ever seen on pop flies. He gets rid of the ball faster than anybody. In a double play he murders the other side. He's always outsmarting the runner. More, he'll get on base for you. Name me a better bunter. He beats you in a dozen ways."

Casey knew the importance of Phil Rizzuto to the Yankees and to their prospects in the pennant race. Casey wanted that pennant as much as any man on the club, on the field or in the front office. He would take care—very good care—of that most valuable Yankee property.

He knew that the Scooter had been hurt most of 1948. He wasn't going to rush him into action.

In spring training, with most everybody trying to impress the new manager, the skipper told Rizzuto to take it easy.

"When you are ready to play ball, let me know," he said to Phil. "Give that arm plenty of rest and don't throw hard for at least a month."

Phil's arm was the key to what kind of season Rizzuto was going to have. All winter long, Phil had followed Dr. Bennett's orders and rested the arm. And, as the doctor ordered, he baked his right elbow every day with heat and diathermy treatments. By March, he was taking a series of arm exercises and each passing day it grew stronger. He finally reached the point when he was experiencing no pain at all when throwing.

"I'd like to try to throw a few balls in a game," he told Casey.

He meant a full nine innings. Stengel had allowed him to play at short in a number of exhibition games, but for only a few innings at a time.

They were scheduled to play the Boston Braves in St. Petersburg on March 31.

"I've got to find out about my arm sometime," said Phil. "Today is as good as any other day."

It was one of the happiest days of his life. In the course of the Yankees' 9–7 victory, Phil was all over the field making the kind of plays that stamped him as one of the great shortstops of all time. He made a number of great throws from deep in the shortstop position, and at the end of the game he was as happy as he had ever been, because his arm felt as good as new.

Stengel, too, was a happy man that day. He couldn't afford another cripple—DiMaggio was ailing, and that could mean the pennant. The Yankee Clipper had undergone an operation in November for the removal of a small bone spur on his right heel and it was once more painful. Joe tried to play, but he could not run very well. He was sent off to Johns Hopkins Hospital in Baltimore for another operation on the foot, and after the operation was performed he was fitted with a special braced shoe. After missing the first sixty-five games of the schedule, Joe finally played his first game on June 28.

On that date the Yankees opened a crucial three-game

series with the Red Sox in Boston, and first place was at stake. The Yankees had held the lead since the first day of the season, but they needed to take at least two of the three games to retain it. DiMaggio played as if the Red Sox series was nothing less than the World Series, hitting four home runs, batting in nine runs, and inspiring the Yankees to a three-game sweep. It was one of the most electrifying individual efforts in baseball history.

There was one big scare for Phil in that same series. Johnny Pesky crashed into him while trying to break up a double play. Pesky's shoulder caught Phil on the jaw and knocked him out. Phil finished the game but he had severe head pains. He missed an appointment the next day for X rays; he had taken sleeping pills and overslept. He skipped the X rays, went directly to the ballpark, and played the whole game despite his aches and pains. And as ill as he was, he saved the game for the Yankees that day.

Ellis Kinder was at bat for the Red Sox. The bases were full. Kinder lined a smash off the glove of the Yankee relief pitcher, Cuddles Marshall, and the ball skidded toward second base as the Red Sox runners rounded the bases. Second baseman Jerry Coleman and Phil went for the ball; it bounced off Jerry's arm. The always alert Rizzuto raced behind second, scooped up the ball, beat the runner coming in from first, then, quick as a bullet, snapped the ball to first, completing a remarkable double play and taking Boston out of a big inning.

"He makes plays Honus Wagner never made," said Stengel, who had seen the legendary Pirate infielder—called by some the greatest in baseball history—while Casey played for the Dodgers.

That was only one of two double plays Rizzuto pulled off that afternoon, despite all the pain he was suffering. He also executed a perfect squeeze bunt that brought home an important run in the Yanks' win over the Red Sox.

Phil did go for X rays the following morning and learned that his jaw was badly bruised but not broken. However, the headaches continued, and in the first inning of the game that day his right arm began to quiver as he went to bat. In the field, his left arm began to shake, as if he had palsy. Immediately Casey had him rushed to the hospital.

The doctors took an electroencephalogram of his brain to determine whether he had a blood clot there.

"They glued twenty-four wires to my hair," said Phil.

There was no clot, but the hospital kept him in bed for a day, to be on the safe side.

"The trembling in your arm is a posttrauma tremor," the doctors explained to the Scooter. "The blow to the jaw induced a slight injury to the nerves. Nothing serious. A few days of rest will take care of everything."

Phil was relieved.

About his bravery as a pivot man in double plays, Cora once pointed out, "Funny how Phil is afraid of worms and eels and mice, and yet he stands up there all the time at second base and isn't afraid at all when those big guys come barreling in at him."

The Yanks had lots of injury problems in 1949. But at least they tried to maintain a sense of humor.

One day at the Stadium Phil was telling a story to Bobby Brown in the dugout, and Stengel, who had been watching the visiting club taking batting practice, turned and asked, "What are you talking about?"

"I was just telling Bobby," Phil explained, "that my wife fell out of bed this morning and . . ."

"Wait a minute," Casey interrupted.

He raised his voice so that players up and down the dugout could hear.

"Listen to this, you guys," he said.

"I was just saying," Phil continued, "that my wife jumped out of bed this morning to pick up the baby, who was crying, and she fell on the floor. She looked so funny I had to laugh. But I felt bad when we found out she'd broken two toes."

"You hear that?" Stengel asked. "Better watch out. This is a rough, tough season. Even our wives are getting hurt."

In September, as the Yankees and Boston Red Sox fought each other tooth and nail, Joe DiMaggio was red hot with his big bat, driving in runs to win the close ones. And Rizzuto held up the infield with his spectacular play. He was all over, cutting off the ball and winging those bullet-like throws over to first to get the speediest base runners. And his timely basehits started rallies and enabled Mapes, Lindell, and Di-Maggio to hit with a man on base.

But September was also a good month for the Red Sox. With Ted Williams and Dom DiMaggio slugging the ball, Boston moved up to take over first place. On September 26, the Sox beat the Yanks in Boston 7–6 in a wild and wooly game. But on September 28, the Yankees pulled even with them. Two days later, in Philadelphia, the Yanks dropped to second by a margin of one game. Then, in a hair-pulling game, they beat the Red Sox on a home run by Johnny Lindell at Yankee Stadium to even up the race. And on October 2, with Phil Rizzuto slashing four hits, including a triple to lead off the game, and Vic Raschi pitching shut-out ball for eight innings, the Yanks won the pennant on the last day of the season.

As the season struggled to a climax Tommy Henrich summed it up best with this statement: "Phil was the solid man on the club. Without him we could have gotten nowhere. We could and did overcome injuries to other players. But if Phil had been lost for any period of time, we would have been sunk, for fair."

Once more the Yankees met the Dodgers in the World Series. In the first game, played at Yankee Stadium, Allie Reynolds and Don Newcombe waged one of the greatest pitching duels in Series history. As the Yankees went to bat in the ninth inning, neither team had scored, Reynolds having yielded two hits and Newcombe just four. Tommy Henrich was first up, and on the third pitch he hammered the ball into the right field stands, and the Yankees won the opener, 1–0.

In the second game the pitchers again dominated the hitters as Vic Raschi and Preacher Roe fought it out. This time it was the Dodger pitcher who won by 1–0, giving up just six hits.

The third game, at Ebbets Field, was another close one as Tommy Byrne dueled Ralph Branca. The score was tied 1–1 in the ninth inning when the Yanks loaded the bases and Johnny Mize singled in two runs. After Coleman and Rizzuto singled, the Yankees had a 4–1 lead, which they barely held on to, winning 4–3.

Allie Reynolds, this time in relief of Eddie Lopat, held the Dodgers in check in the fourth game as Bobby Brown emerged as the hero with a double and bases-filled triple as the Yankees won 6–4.

The Series concluded with a slugfest as the Yankees pounded six Dodger hurlers. Rizzuto punched a single in the first inning and came through with a two-base hit in the third as the Yankees won the finale, 10–6.

There was talk of the Scooter being named Most Valuable Player in the American League for 1949. He didn't get the award, though he did poll 175 points. But Ted Williams, the great Bosox slugger, got 273 points and the award.

Phil did not conceal his disappointment.

"Not that I wasn't glad to see Williams get it," he said. "I just felt that a little guy like myself would never get another chance at the big prize. It only happens once to a fellow in my position, I figured. It was tough to come so close. I couldn't believe I'd ever have another year like that one, and even if I did, somebody like Joe DiMaggio or Ted Williams would have a better one."

The New York sportswriters made up a bit for this disappointment at their annual dinner at the Waldorf-Astoria in February 1950. They awarded the Scooter the Sid Mercer Memorial Award as Player of the Year.

Some people saw the award as a sort of consolation prize for the little fellow, but anybody who cared to scan the records for 1949 could see that he had more than earned it.

In 1949 the Scooter had led the New York Yankees in games played, in hits, runs, doubles, stolen bases, and total bases. He led the league's shortstops with a .971 fielding percentage.

It was a great year for Phil Rizzuto, but greater things were still to come in 1950.

A young Phil Rizzuto trying to make the grade at spring training in St. Petersburg, Florida, February 1941. Note the type of glove then in use.

Newbold Morris, New York City council president, presents little Phil with a tall trophy, the minor league Most Valuable Player award, which he won after a great year with Kansas City in 1940. Yankee teammates and Cleveland Indians look on before their July 23, 1941, game.

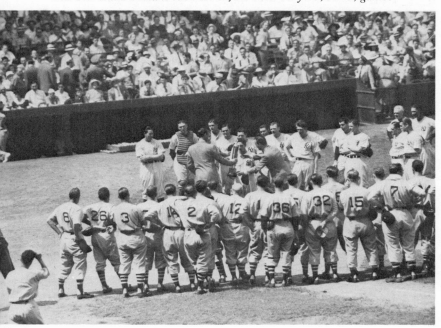

Phil, attending Yankee Stadium in his Navy garb, watches game two of the New York vs. St. Louis World Series during a furlough on October 6, 1943. With him is the Cardinals' Terry Moore.

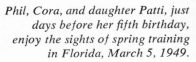

Phil, Cora, and daughter Patti, just days before her fifth birthday, enjoy the sights of spring training in Florida, March 5, 1949.

The ball's nowhere in sight and the Scooter scores the first run in this August 15, 1949, game against the Philadelphia Athletics. Catcher Mickey Guerra waits for the late throw.

The Old Professor, Casey Stengel, celebrates the first of many pennants. A 5-3 win over Boston did the trick on October 2, 1949, and Phil, who scored the first run for the Yanks after a lead-off triple, gets a big victory hug.

World Series action in game four of the 1949 battle against the Dodgers. Here Phil tries to avoid a tag by catcher Roy Campanella in the first inning after Yogi Berra grounded to third. Umpire Art Passarela, however, called the Scooter out for going out of the baseline.

That magic bunt. Phil lays a beauty down to advance Vic Raschi from second to third base in a May 1952 game against the Indians. Catcher is Birdie Tebbetts.

Poetry in motion, as the Scooter might say. After taking the throw from Billy Martin, Phil leaps gracefully on his double-play pivot to avoid the Indians' Larry Doby in this September 13, 1953, game.

Out of uniform and up in the booth, ex-shortstop Rizzuto does the play-by-play on April 15, 1957.

Still scootin' after all those years, Phil takes the field on Old Timers Day, August 11, 1968. Former Yankee first baseman Joe Pepitone films the action.

13

MVP—
Most Valuable Phil

Casey Stengel made some key changes in the Yankee club when he took over as manager of the Yankees. In 1949, George McQuinn was gone, and Tommy Henrich was moved from the outfield to first base. Snuffy Stirnweiss was traded to the St. Louis Browns and the rookie Jerry Coleman sent in to play second. At third, Billy Johnson was gone and Bobby Brown, the medical student, brought up from Newark, played the bag. Charlie Keller was traded to the Detroit Tigers. Casey had three new boys in the outfield, Hank Bauer, Gene Woodling, and Cliff Mapes. Hank Bauer, the ex-Marine who had fought in the battle of Okinawa, came up from Kansas. Gene Woodling had been the Player of the Year in the Pacific Coast League, where he had hit .385 for the San Francisco club. Cliff Mapes was the strong boy all the scouts were touting as the next Babe Ruth. Johnny Mize, who had been the slugging hero of the St. Louis Cardinals for so many years, joined the Yankees late in '49, at the age of thirty-six.

There weren't that many changes in 1950, but Casey did bring up a pitcher in late June who was to become one of the game's great sensations, that year and for many years to come—Whitey Ford.

Ford had been a fine pitcher for Manhattan Aviation High School in New York, a vocational high school, and then became one of the outstanding sandlot pitchers in the New York area. In October 1946 Whitey was signed by Yankee scout Paul Krichell for a $7,000 bonus and was sent to Binghamton in the spring of 1947. He was there for just one month when his manager, former Yankee pitcher Lefty Gomez, sent him to the Yankee farm team in Butler. Ford spent three years in the minors, pitching impressively each year and moving up the baseball ladder after each successful season.

In 1949 Whitey won 16 and lost 5 games with Binghamton, and while the Yankees were struggling to beat Boston for the pennant that year, Ford phoned Casey Stengel and confidently told him he was available and could help win the pennant for the Yanks. He was 21 years old, brash and cocky, when he was brought up by Casey in 1950.

Curiously enough, the baseball writers didn't pick the Yanks to repeat their 1949 triumph; they figured the Boston Red Sox would take the 1950 pennant, and, as the season began, there was every reason to believe they had made the right guess.

Joe DiMaggio was again ailing. He had fully intended to end his playing days after the 1949 World Series, but Dan Topping, one of the new owners of the Yankees, had pleaded with him to stay on. Joe felt he owed Topping and the Yankees something, and he agreed to return to the New York fold. But his heel bothered him so much that it was almost impossible for him to swing the bat. In the early going of the 1950 season, DiMaggio wasn't producing at all, and the Jolter's batting average was on the worst skid of his career.

There were other woes for the Yankee skipper. Tommy

Henrich had slowed down, and he couldn't get his big bat around on those fastballs. The rookie, Joe Collins, replacing Henrich at first, was having a miserable time at the bat. Hank Bauer seriously injured an ankle. Even the Scooter had some serious physical difficulty. In spring training his throwing arm hurt so bad that all he could do was lob the ball to first base.

But even so it was the Scooter, with his fielding and his bat, who was to carry the New York Yankees through most, if not all, of the 1950 season. Everyone expected Phil's marvels in the field, but he amazed them, and perhaps himself, with his performance at the plate in that glorious year.

In the first six weeks of the 1950 season, the Scooter hit everything pitched at him, batting at a mighty clip of .355. He led the Yankees to eight straight wins on their first western trip of the season with an astounding batting average of .441. It got so that the fans began to expect so much of the Scooter's bat that they almost forgot he was the best fielding shortstop in the American League. When he broke the American League record for consecutive errorless games played by a shortstop —a record set in 1949 by Eddie Joost of the Philadelphia Athletics of 42 games and 226 chances without a boot—in a contest with the Cleveland Indians on May 22, the fans hardly took notice of it. He had played every game of the season to date so flawlessly, without muffing one play, that the fans had come to take that kind of performance for granted. The Scooter's string continued for another two weeks, and his new league marks stood at 289 chances and 58 games without error.

The pitchers began to notice the Scooter's prowess at the plate. The little guy was actually hitting for a higher average than all the Yankee sluggers, and for the first time

in his career, Phil had to be alert and ready for the "duster."
They were throwing the ball hard, high, and tight, sometimes
a bit too close to his head. The idea was to loosen him up at
the plate and prevent him from taking a toe-hold. Phil may
have feared mice and eels and such, but he was fearless on
the field, taking in stride the punishment inflicted by all those
big bruisers barreling into him at second base. He wasn't
about to be scared by any pitcher in the league, no matter
how fast and close he hurled that baseball.

Casey Stengel, as always, appreciated the job Phil was
doing for the Yankees. In 1949 Rizzuto had been just beaten
in the All Star vote by Eddie Joost; this year Casey wasn't
going to let anything get between the Scooter and the All Star
game. He began an all-out campaign to be sure that Phil got
the votes he had failed to get in 1949. There wasn't a time he
spoke to the writers covering baseball—and he spoke to them
often—that he didn't put in a plug for his shortstop.

"I've seen some great boys in the short field in my time,"
said the Old Professor, "but none of them ever did anything
Phil has not shown this year. In fact, I would call my boy 'Mr.
Shortstop' because I cannot conceive of a better showing by
Reese, Marion [Marty, the great Cardinal shortstop], or any
other shortstop in the game."

And when Casey Stengel spoke of his "Mr. Shortstop" it
was in straightforward English, not in his legendary Stengelese,
the run-on, confusing way he had of talking to the press or
even his own team. What could be clearer than this testi-
monial: "If I were a retired gentleman, I would follow the
Yankees around just to see Rizzuto work those miracles
every day."

There was one time, when the team was traveling from New

York to Boston, that Casey talked for five hours straight about "Mr. Shortstop" to the sportswriters who accompanied the Yankees on the trip.

"So he won't hit the long ball like Stephens [Vern, who hit 30 homers in 1950 for the Red Sox] or Joost," Casey declaimed. "But show me anything else he can't do better. He's the fastest shortstop in the league. He covers the most ground. He is the most accurate thrower. He has the surest hands.

"He is the key man in the infield," continued the skipper. "No shortstop alive can make as many 'impossible' plays as Rizzuto. And did you ever see anybody with his speed and ability on the double play?

"He's the best bunter in baseball," Casey continued. "He bunts with thought and precision. And he can put that ball down on any spot for the squeeze play."

The skipper would remind his audience of the eight straight wins with which the Yankees had opened the season, then add, "And Phil squeezed home the winning run in two of those eight games!"

There was no doubt at all about Phil Rizzuto's artistry at laying down the perfect bunt. Players glued their eyes on the little guy, trying to learn his magical technique.

Phil was a right-handed batter. He would stand there at the plate, in his regular batting stance, from all appearances getting ready for a full swing at the pitch. But suddenly he would slide his right hand up on the bat, pull his left elbow tight against his body, present the bat, which was now parallel to the ground, to the pitch, and catch the ball right on the fat part of the bat. His hind foot would come forward as he met the ball, and he would be off to first base before the ball hit the ground.

Mickey Mantle was to say of the way Phil had bunting down to a science, "It was really a delight to watch Phil bunt, a delight to nearly everybody but the pitcher. I never saw anyone, before or since, who could bunt the way Phil did."

"The fans are nuts if they don't vote Phil Rizzuto All Star," barked Casey. "And tell them I said so!"

Casey Stengel wasn't alone in singing praises of the Scooter. Any number of managers, ball players, and others added to the chorus of voices lauding the brilliance of the Yankee star shortstop.

"Rizzuto is unquestionably the best shortstop in our league," claimed Lou Boudreau, at that time manager of the Cleveland Indians.

Lou Boudreau knew a bit about shortstops. As an active ballplayer, he had played shortstop on five American League All Star teams, and he became a Hall of Famer in 1970.

"I'd like to have him on any team I had anything to do with," said Hank Greenberg, the all-time great slugger and then the front office boss of the Indians. "He can do more with his ability and equipment than any shortstop I've ever seen."

Vic Raschi, known as the Springfield Rifle, one of the Yankees' ace pitchers, said, "It's nice to turn around and see that little guy at shortstop. He makes pitching that much easier." And on another occasion he paid a grand compliment by saying, "My best pitch is anything the batter grounds, lines, or pops in the direction of Rizzuto."

Tom Ferrick, the veteran relief pitcher, came to the Yankees from the St. Louis Browns in mid-June 1950. He had won one game and lost three with the Browns. He turned in an eight and four record for the New York club. Asked what made the difference, he explained, "In St. Louis when a batter hit a hard ball into the infield, by the time I turned around the ball was already in the outfield for a hit. With the Yankees, I just turn around and watch Rizzuto and Coleman reel off a double play. Rizzuto gets the balls that go by other short-stops. That's the main reason why pitching for the Yankees is such a good deal."

It's impossible to say how much all those kudos helped in the All-Star balloting, or whether Phil Rizzuto even needed them. His play in the field and at the plate had the entire baseball world focused on him. And with Casey putting a bug in the sportswriters' ears, and the writers duly reporting on the Scooter's sparkling play, the fans overwhelmingly elected him to the American League team. Phil played the entire game and got two hits in six at bats in the fourteen-inning thriller that wound up 4–3 in favor of the National League squad. Better things were still in store for the Scooter in 1950.

Phil had credited Al Kunitz, his old high school coach, with teaching him the rudiments of the game. He had credited Ray White with helping him develop his skills down in Norfolk and Bassett. He credited Joe Gordon and especially Frank Crosetti for the advice and instruction they gave him when he came up with the Yankees, and Joe McCarthy for teaching him all the finer points of the game. However high the Scooter climbed in the baseball world, he never lost his innate modesty; he never failed to give credit where it was due. He credited the veteran Johnny Mize with teaching him to be more patient and more selective as a hitter, which was a big factor in his success at bat in 1950.

"I used to grip my bat too hard," the Scooter explained. "I was so anxious to get hits that I was too tense. It made me commit myself and sock at balls that I should have let go by.

Mize noticed that at batting practice, when we were in spring training, and suggested I loosen my grip and relax.

"I did just that, with Johnny Mize watching me. I spread my stance at the plate. I widened the distance between my feet. It helped."

There was more.

"Johnny Mize handed me his bat," said the Scooter. "He said, 'Go ahead and try it.' I did, and it worked. The only thing I had to do was to ask the manufacturer to reduce the size and weight of the bat, so I'd feel more comfortable with it. Yeah," concluded the Scooter, "Johnny Mize and his bat certainly started me off on a good streak, didn't they?"

Appreciative and modest, always modest—that was Phil. When someone called his attention to the fact that he was the last of the "old" Yankees, with DiMaggio and Henrich playing out their careers, he commented: "I don't belong in the same class, much less the same breath, with those guys." Just mentioning "those guys" was enough to bring a note of awe into the Scooter's voice. "Jeepers," he said, "I'm lucky to be on the same team with them."

Phil wasn't putting on an act. As honest as he was modest, he never said anything he didn't believe.

The Yankees clinched the 1950 pennant on September 29. Phil closed the season as the top Yankee hitter with an average of .324, two hundred hits, thirty-six of which were doubles, seven triples, and seven home runs. He finished sixth in the race for the American League batting title. And once again he was the best fielding shortstop in the league, with a .982 fielding average. It came as a surprise to no one when the Baseball Writers' Association voted Rizzuto the Most Valuable Player in the American League for 1950.

The only one surprised was Phil, though why he should have been so surprised no one can say.

"Me?" he almost hollered. "No! There must be better players in the league than me!"

Apparently the sportswriters didn't think so. Sixteen of the twenty-three writers voted him first place on their MVP ballots; five, second; one, third; and one, fourth for a total of 284 points. The American League batting champion of the year, the Red Sox's Billy Goodman, came in second in the balloting, collecting 180 points. Yogi Berra came in third with 146. It was the Scooter, no doubt about it, by a well-earned landslide.

Phil picked up other honors that year. He was named the Best Dressed Athlete of 1950 by the Clothing Institute of America. He was voted the Most Popular Yankee of 1950 by the fans in the Bronx who responded to a contest by the *Bronx Home News*, a distinction that carried with it the gift of an Austin sedan. Phil lived in New Jersey, and the state named him the Outstanding New Jersey Athlete of the Year. He was awarded the $10,000 jewel-studded belt, the Hickok Award, as the Outstanding Professional Athlete of 1950.

Perhaps the award Phil enjoyed receiving most that year came just about a month before his third child, Penelope Ann, was born. In June 1950 he was named Sports Father of the Year.

The World Series was anticlimactic, for Phil, for the Yankees, and for all of baseball. The Philadelphia Phillies, the Whiz Kids, won the National League pennant on the last day of the season in a thrilling extra-inning game against the Dodgers. Worn down, perhaps, by the long, grueling season, the Phillies dropped four in a row to the Yanks, who were led to victory by the strong pitching of Vic Raschi, Allie Reynolds, Tom Ferrick, and Whitey Ford. Phil didn't have much of a Series—two hits in fourteen trips to the plate and one stolen base—but he was flawless in the field.

1950 was the greatest year in Phil Rizzuto's career. It was a year in which he received all the recognition he deserved from the fans, the players, the managers, and the top baseball brass. There would never be another like it for the Scooter, unquestionably now one of the greatest shortstops in the history of the game.

14

As Indispensable
as Ever

In 1951 the United States was involved in the Korean War, and young men were again being drafted for service in the Armed Forces. The brilliant rookie, Whitey Ford, who in 1950 had won nine games for the Yankees while losing only one, was in Army uniform before the '51 season could get under way. Jerry Coleman and Bobby Brown were drafted and went into the service before the season was over.

Casey Stengel had other problems as well at the start of the new season. Joe DiMaggio was thirty-six years old and had played in 1950 only because he felt he owed it to Dan Topping. Phil Rizzuto had had the greatest year of his career in 1950, but he wasn't getting any younger. The Scooter was thirty-two years old, and his sore arm continued to plague him. Phil still had a couple of good years left, but Casey needed to plan ahead. Case also knew that the more he could rest the Scooter, the longer he would have him in the field.

Tommy Henrich, who had retired from the game, said to a sportswriter about the Yankees, "Don't worry. They'll be all right without me. But they're going to be in trouble if they lose Phil."

Casey Stengel knew that well. Shopping for men to take up the baseball battles for the older players whose careers were waning, he concentrated especially on men who might play shortstop.

Stengel instituted an instructional camp in Phoenix, Arizona, in February 1951, and he collected a fine group of young prospects. There was Andy Carey, a nineteen-year-old bonus baby. Also in attendance were twenty-year-old Tom Sturdivant, a fine pitching prospect, and Gil McDougald, the Most Valuable Player in the Texas League in 1950. And there was a nineteen-year-old youngster by the name of Mickey Mantle, who had been voted the Most Valuable Player in the Western Association in 1950.

Mickey Charles Mantle, born in Spavinaw, Oklahoma, on October 20, 1931, was destined to become a ballplayer if ever a man was. His father, Elvin, a miner, and his grandfather, Charles, had been semipro players. Mickey was named for Mickey Cochrane, the great catcher for the Philadelphia Athletics and Detroit Tigers, who was his father's idol. When he was two years old, his dad clapped a baseball cap on Mickey's head and put a miniature bat in his hands. And as soon as he was big enough to swing a stick, he took batting practice every night, hitting left-handed and then switching over to a right-handed stance.

The day he graduated from high school, Mickey's dad signed a Yankee contract for him, receiving a $1500 bonus, and Mickey was farmed out to the Independence club of the Kansas-Oklahoma League. There, as a shortstop in eighty-nine games, he hit .313. For the 1950 season he was sent up to Joplin and led the Western Association with a .383 average.

And from the day Mickey walked out on the field in

Phoenix he was a sensation. Batting right- or left-handed, he hit the ball out of sight. He ran like a sprinter and easily won all the foot races in camp. He overshadowed even Joe Di-Maggio. Stories about him and his incredible play streamed over the wires, and scores of pictures of him appeared in the newspapers and weekly news magazines. Even the other ball-players shook their heads in wonder at his almost-incredible feats.

"I never in all my life saw anybody like him," said Di-Maggio.

Reporters asked Stengel about his newest sensation, and Casey responded, "They see him a few times and they ask me what I'm going to do about him. Well, he's a shortstop, but he ain't going to get Rizzuto out of there. Nobody in the whole world can move my little Scooter. I try him in right field and he misjudges balls. One of them hits him on the head. But he can hit and he can run. We'll have to see what we can do with him."

There were others at the camp. There was the 20-year-old kid out of Purdue University, Bill (Moose) Skowron. There was Bob Cerv. And there was a kid pitcher by the name of Tom Morgan. Morgan was to win nine games for the Yankees in 1951.

McDougald was the best shortstop prospect in camp, and in time he would play that position for the New York club, but no one could take the Scooter's place, not just yet. Phil was still the sparkplug for the Yankees. He was still the great in-fielder, the double-play maker, the man who could bring the winning run home with the suicide squeeze. It was such a bunt that sent DiMaggio home with the winning run in the bottom of the ninth to beat the Cleveland Indians on September 17,

1951. It was a key Yankee win that put the New York club at the head of the American League pennant race by one full game over the Indians. It was a lead the Yanks held the rest of the way to win the third straight pennant for Casey Stengel.

The losing pitcher in that victory over Cleveland that day, incidentally, was Bob Lemon. Lemon would later come over to the New York club to pilot it to a pennant and World Series victory in 1978 and another pennant in 1981.

The Yanks had taken four straight to become World Champions in 1950. In 1951, the story would be somewhat different; they were up against a miracle team in the New York Giants.

Leo Durocher was the skipper of the New York National League team. In the middle of August 1951, the Giants were a full thirteen and a half games behind the mighty Brooklyn Dodgers. No one figured that anyone could catch up. Certainly no one figured any club could possibly beat them out of the National League pennant. Nobody, that is, except Lippy Leo Durocher.

It was a kid by the name of Willie Mays who caught fire and sparked an unbelievable dash to the wire in 1951. He robbed batters of base hits with his spectacular play in the outfield. He cut down runners on the basepaths with his terrific arm. His prowess at the bat was to become legendary. Of their last forty-four games that year, the Giants, led by Mays, won thirty-seven, enough to finish in a tie for the lead at the end of the regulation season. A three-game set-to was scheduled between the Dodgers and Giants, the winner of two of those games to go into the World Series.

The New York Giants had a few other star ballplayers in

addition to Willie Mays. There were Whitey Lockman, Eddie Stanky, Alvin Dark, Monte Irvin, and the Scotsman Bobby Thomson. They also had two twenty-three-game winners in pitchers Larry Jansen and the Barber, Sal Maglie; and Wes Westrum was a crackerjack catcher. It was a top-flight baseball club that had just been a little slow getting started in 1951.

The Giants and Dodgers split the first two games of that mini-series to decide the National League championship. However, the Giants' chance of victory seemed slight in the bottom half of the final inning of that third and deciding game.

The Giants came up in the ninth in a do-or-die situation—the Dodgers were leading 4–1 and seemed headed for victory and the championship. But the Giants managed to get one run in and had two men on base with only one out when Ralph Branca came out of the bullpen to relieve flagging starter Don Newcombe. Bobby Thomson came to the plate to face Branca.

Branca's first pitch to Thomson was a good one, but Bobby took it for a strike. The fans groaned. Would Thomson get another pitch like that to hit?

The second pitch wasn't like the first. It was a high, inside fastball, a tough pitch to hit. But Thomson met it and sent a low liner to left field that stayed high enough to clear the wall by a matter of inches.

There it was, "the shot heard 'round the world," "the miracle of Coogan's Bluff." The Giant fans, after a stunned moment, went wild.

Three men crossed the plate. The New York Giants, with a last gasp home run off the bat of Bobby Thomson, had defeated the Dodgers, 5–4, and sent the deliriously happy gang of Giants running for their lives from the equally deliriously happy fans.

There was pandemonium in the locker room. The New York Giants were the National League champions!

It was expected that the Yankees would sweep the 1951 Series, as they had swept the Series of 1950. The Giants, after all, had had a grueling season, topped off by a dramatic three-game series. They were supposed to be tired, washed up, after all the drama and emotion they had experienced in getting to the top. And among others on the Yankees pitching staff, they had to hit against Allie Reynolds, who had pitched two no-hit games in 1951.

But the Giants didn't lie down. They won the first game of the World Series handily, 5–1, and beat the Yankee ace, Allie Reynolds, to do it. They also took the third game of the fall classic, beating Vic Raschi, another of the Yankee aces, in the process.

But that was all. Behind in the Series, with one win against two losses, the Yanks took command and swept the next three games for the world championship.

For the third time in three years, Casey Stengel had piloted the New York Yankees to the top of the heap, winning the American League pennant and then the world championship. It was a very happy Casey who led his team back to the locker room. Almost every man in a Yankee uniform was just as exultant. But there was one exception. As everyone else poured champagne and celebrated, Joe DiMaggio stood quietly in front of his locker.

After a while, he took off his shirt and opened a bottle of beer.

The sportswriters were all around him, firing questions at him.

DiMaggio had only one statement to give them.

"I've played my final game," he said. "I've played my final game."

No one, not even Dan Topping, was going to dissuade him from retiring this time.

As for the Scooter, there wasn't a doubt in his mind about his plans for next year, or the year after, or any of the years after that. Sure, 1951 hadn't been the year he had had in 1950. His batting average had dropped fifty points, but his .274 was more than respectable for a man playing shortstop. And he had led the Yankees in the World Series in hits (8) and runs (5). His batting average of .320 was second only to Bobby Brown's .357. And he even collected his second Series homer in game five.

In fact, Phil was one of the heroes of the 1951 classic. His fielding was, as always, magnificent. The roughhousing Eddie Stanky did drop-kick the ball out of the Scooter's glove on a particularly vicious slide into second base during the third game, which opened the door to a five-run fifth inning, but the little shortstop more than made up for that infamous incident. He inaugurated or participated in eight of the ten double plays executed by the Yanks in the six-game Series.

The Scooter was dead-tired at the end of the 1951 season. He had celebrated his thirty-third birthday in September of that year. But even the youngest ballplayer needs a rest after the punishment of the long season and then postseason play; the fierce competition, the pressure, the enormous energy that is expended every day, all take their toll on a major leaguer. Phil was no exception. But if anybody thought that the Scooter was approaching the end of his career on the diamond, it wasn't Phil Rizzuto.

Phil was encouraged by his outstanding Series performance.

It made up considerably for the disappointing batting average he had compiled during the regular season. But that disappointment was quickly forgotten by the Scooter. He began to look forward to a better year in 1952, perhaps a year that would be as good as 1950 had been.

15

The Scooter
Meets Billy the Kid

1952 is remembered by many fans as the year Billy Martin emerged as a full-fledged Yankee and the year of Mickey Mantle's tape-measure home runs. And the Yankee Clipper, Joe DiMaggio, had kept his promise and finally retired, making the official announcement in December 1951, ending a special era of Yankee baseball.

Billy Martin was Stengel's pet, as scrappy a young player as Casey had been in his heyday. He had played for Casey when Stengel managed the Oakland Acorns to the Pacific Coast League championship in 1948, and he had been up and down with the Yankees since 1950. In 1952 he took over second base chores for Jerry Coleman, who spent most of the year in the military service.

Martin, who grew up tough in the Bay area in California, was a combative young man. He didn't need to be goaded into a fight; his fists were always ready to put an end to any argument in which he was involved.

Jimmy Piersall, a rookie with the Boston Red Sox, learned about Billy's temper the hard way in a game in 1952.

"Hey, Pinocchio!" he yelled at Billy, who does have a rather pronounced nose. "Wanna fight?"

Billy Martin obliged. Piersall and Martin met after the game and, before any of the other ballplayers could prevent the mayhem, Billy had floored Piersall with two hard, vicious rights to his head.

He took care of Clint Courtney, the St. Louis Browns' catcher, with a right to the head, when that particularly belligerent player came after him bent on destruction during a game in 1953. He took care of Courtney another time, too; this time in defense of the Scooter.

At St. Louis, in a tight game between the Yankees and the Browns, Courtney came to bat in the bottom of the tenth inning. Courtney was mad. In the top of the frame McDougald had bowled him over at the plate, forcing the catcher to lose the ball and scoring the go-ahead run for the Yanks, the run that would win the game for them.

Courtney, first up at bat, turned to Yogi Berra and said, "Someone is going to pay for that. No one is going to bowl me over and get away with it."

He got good wood on the ball and slashed it to right. A clean single. There wasn't a chance of his stretching the hit into a double, but he headed straight for second base, anyway.

Phil was straddling the bag, the ball in his glove, ready to tag Courtney out. Everyone in the park knew what Courtney was up to, especially the other Yankees. Allie Reynolds, Joe Collins, Hank Bauer, Gil McDougald, and Billy Martin charged from their positions in the field toward second base. No one was going to hurt Phil Rizzuto, not if they could help it.

But they got there too late. Courtney slid into the bag,

spikes flashing, and caught the little guy on the right leg, gashing it badly in two places.

Collins and McDougald took a swing at Courtney. Allie Reynolds grabbed the big catcher and pinned down his arms. Billy Martin delivered the *coup de grâce*. He hit the bully square in the face, knocking off his glasses and drawing blood. Bob Cerv, the burly Yankee outfielder, finished the job by stomping on Courtney's glasses, smashing them to smithereens.

Martin's pugilistic antics brought him a great deal of notoriety, and continue to do so today. But he distinguished himself in other, more important ways during 1952. In fact, he would turn out to be one of the Yankee heroes of the year.

The Yanks got off to a slow start in the pennant race. Sluggers Yogi Berra, Hank Bauer, and Gene Woodling were having trouble at the plate. Pitchers Eddie Lopat and Vic Raschi were on the sidelines for a spell, Lopat with a sore arm and Raschi with a knee injury. Phil was having the usual arm problems during the early going, and Mickey Mantle's knee wasn't in the best of shape. To add to Casey Stengel's difficulties, along with Jerry Coleman, Bobby Brown and pitcher Tom Morgan were scooped up by the military.

The Cleveland Indians jumped out to a quick lead behind the magnificent pitching of Bob Lemon, Early Wynn, and Mike Garcia, all of whom went on to win twenty or more games that year. Al Rosen, Larry Doby, and Dale Mitchell led the offensive attack.

But Casey the miracle worker, against what seemed to be impossible odds, pulled the Yanks out of their nosedive, and they took over the league lead on June 9 on a four-hit pitching effort over the Tigers by Lopat. The Indians stayed close, though, and the Yanks' lead on Labor Day was a slim 2½ games. Finally, on September 26, in an extra-inning game against the Athletics, Billy Martin hammered home two runs to help the Yanks clinch the pennant. Casey and the Yanks had won the long struggle and were proud owners of their fourth straight American League flag.

It had been a tough battle, with every game crucial and demanding the best that Casey could field for the Yankees. Phil, thirty-four years old in September, could have used a couple of days off to rest his aching arms and legs, but Old Case couldn't afford to have him on the bench, ever, with the outcome of every game so important to the pennant race. The Scooter played in 152 games in 1952. Of all the other Yankees, only twenty-four-year-old Gil McDougald played in as many. Phil was going to pay for that long stretch of games, and Casey Stengel knew it, but the Skipper needed the Scooter's sure hands at shortstop, his quickness in turning over double plays, and his bat. Phil didn't have a great year at the plate, hitting only .254, but he was a clutch hitter and still the greatest bunter in the league. And, as in years past, he was among the league leaders in stolen bases with seventeen.

Then there was the World Series, and Casey certainly wasn't going to let the Scooter sit out the battle for the world championship.

The World Series of 1952 was another of those classic struggles between the Brooklyn Dodgers and the New York Yankees. As usual it would go down to the wire. This year it was to have an extraordinarily dramatic finish, with Billy Martin emerging as the Yankee hero.

At Ebbets Field for game one, the rookie Dodger pitcher

Joe Black took the measure of the Yankees, 4–2, and became the first black pitcher to record a Series win. The Yanks came back to win the second game, 7–1, Vic Raschi's three-hit pitching aided by Billy Martin's three-run homer that broke open the game in the sixth inning. Preacher Roe pitched the third game of the classic, in Yankee Stadium, and beat the Bombers, 5–3. Then Allie Reynolds squared things again, giving up only four hits and blanking the Dodgers 2–0.

The fifth game was sensational. The Dodgers tagged Ewell Blackwell for one run in the second inning and three in the fifth, opening up a 4–0 lead. Blackwell, a fastball pitcher with a mean disposition, had come to the Yankees late in the '52 season. His bread-and-butter pitch was the inside fastball, close to the head. When he had pitched for the Cincinnati Reds, he had always been effective against the Dodgers. Not so in this fifth game of the World Series.

But the Yankees answered with five runs of their own in the bottom of the fifth, as the veteran Johnny Mize hit a three-run homer.

Duke Snider, that celebrated Dodger, who had hit a two-run homer in the Dodger fifth, then singled home the tying run in the seventh. And it was the Duke who singled in the winning run for the Brooklyn club in the eleventh inning, to the consternation of the fans in Yankee Stadium. The Dodgers had the lead in the Series, three games to two. One more game and at last they would have the New Yorkers beaten, and the World Championship, which they had never won. To make the situation more dismal for the Yankee fans, the fall classic was going back to Ebbets Field, the Dodgers' home turf.

The sixth game was another beauty. The Dodgers had Billy Loes on the mound; the Yankees sent in Vic Raschi. Both were stingy, but the hero of the fifth game, Duke Snider, belted two of Raschi's pitches for home runs. Luckily for Raschi and the Yanks, the bases were empty both times. For the Yanks, both Yogi Berra and Mickey Mantle belted homers, Mantle's blast in the eighth proving to be the winning run in that crucial sixth game. Vic Raschi contributed to the 3–2 victory by bouncing a single off Loes's knee in the seventh inning to send Gene Woodling in from second.

Once again the Series was tied. The championship had come down to the seventh and final game. This was the game that was to produce the single most dramatic moment of the year.

Casey sent Eddie Lopat to the mound. That was a gamble. Eddie was a left-handed pitcher and southpaws didn't fare too well in Ebbets Field, where a low left field wall tempted right-handed hitters. Charlie Dressen, the Dodger skipper, sent in Joe Black again.

There was no scoring in the first three innings.

In the fourth, the Scooter drove a hard-hit ball between Billy Cox, the Dodger third baseman, and the third base line for a double. Johnny Mize singled him home, and the Yanks had the early lead, 1–0.

But the Dodgers came back in their half of the fourth. The Duke singled. Jackie Robinson and the great catcher, Roy Campanella, followed with two surprise drag bunts. The bases were full of Brooklyns, and no one out!

Eddie Lopat was through for the day.

The Dodger fans were up on their feet, cheering, all set for a big inning that would finish the Yanks.

Allie Reynolds came in to pitch for New York. The first man he had to face was Gil Hodges. Hodges had one of the mightiest bats in baseball, but he had gone hitless in seventeen at bats in the Series. He had all of Brooklyn going to church, praying for their great first-baseman in his travail, praying for the Lord to give him back his hitting prowess.

Gil Hodges swung his bat. It was a sharp line drive, but right at Gene Woodling in left. One out. But the Duke came in with a run to tie the score.

Reynolds, though, was a cool customer. He threw three strikes at George (Shotgun) Shuba. Two out. Then he forced the dangerous Carl Furillo to bounce to McDougald at third, and the Dodgers were through—for that inning anyway. The Yankees had escaped possible disaster.

The fans in the stands sat down quietly. The stands grew still quieter when Gene Woodling got hold of a Joe Black pitch in the top of the fifth and sent it into Bedford Avenue, beyond right field. But again the Dodgers evened the score in the bottom of the frame on a double by Cox and a single by Peewee Reese.

The high drama was yet to come.

Mickey Mantle hit one over the right-field scoreboard in the sixth inning to put the Yanks in front again.

In the seventh, McDougald singled. Rizzuto, up for the third time, laid down a perfect bunt, and then beat the throw to first base. Mantle singled in a run and that was the end of the Yankee scoring for the afternoon.

Casey lifted Reynolds and put in Vic Raschi to pitch the seventh, hoping he'd protect the 4–2 Yankee lead. But Raschi had pitched seven and two-thirds innings just the day before, and his arm was not quite equal to the task.

He walked the first batter, Carl Furillo. He got Rocky Nelson to pop up, but Cox singled and Peewee Reese walked. For the second time in the game the bases were loaded with Dodgers.

Stengel walked out to the mound again. Reynolds was finished for the Series. The skipper waved in Bob Kuzava, a surprise. Kuzava was a southpaw, too, and he had to face the Duke and Jackie Robinson, two of the biggest guns in the Dodger arsenal.

Duke Snider swung his bat menacingly at the plate and forced the count to 3 and 2, but Kuzava tied the slugger up, and all he could do was pop up.

Now there were two away, but the bases were still loaded and the man with the bat was the always-dangerous Jackie Robinson. Jackie could hurt a pitcher in many ways. He could find a hole in the infield. He could smash the ball against or over the wall in right, center, or left. He could also drag a bunt better than almost anybody else in baseball, and he was one of the fastest men on the bases. Jackie Robinson was a challenge at all times; he was a special challenge with three men on, two out, and the Dodgers just one run behind the Yankees.

Kuzava pitched him carefully, to another full count, and with the next pitch, Furillo, Cox, and Reese were off, running around the bases. Then, like Snider before him, Jackie popped the ball up. But, unlike Snider's popup, this wasn't going to be an easy out.

Kuzava got out of the way, as far away from the play as possible. Someone else in the infield would have to catch that ball.

When there is a pop that climbs up into the sky as Robinson's did, it is the job of the catcher to call for the man to make the play. That's what Yogi Berra did.

"Collins!" he shouted. "Collins!"

But Collins, playing first, couldn't see the ball. It was up in the sun, and Joe just stood at his bag and didn't move an inch.

Carl Furillo and Billy Cox had already crossed home plate. Peewee Reese was rounding third, headed for home with the lead run.

But Billy Martin, that aggressive sandlot kid, saw that Collins had been blinded by the sun; he also quickly recognized that no one else was going after that tall pop that Jackie Robinson had lifted skyward.

Quicker than he could say "Jack Robinson," Billy Martin went after the popup. He raced behind the mound, and as the wind carried the ball away from him, he lunged for it and made the grab, the momentum of the chase bringing him to his knees.

It was one of the most spectacular catches in World Series history. And it saved the game for the Yankees, giving the New York club its fourth world championship in a row with Casey Stengel at the helm.

There was good reason to celebrate, but it had been a tense year, a hard year, and some of the veterans paid for it.

The 1952 season hadn't been the best for the Scooter. His batting average fell to .254, seventy points below his career high in 1950. But he had been as reliable as ever in the field, leading American League shortstops in assists and double plays, and continued to be the club's sparkplug. At the age of thirty-four, he should have been permitted some respite by his skipper. He should have been taken out of a game now and then, just to be rested. Even an inning or two on the bench might have been helpful. But the race for the pennant had been close, too close to allow Casey the luxury of resting "Mr. Shortstop." And the World Series had been too tight an affair as well. The Scooter played in all but two of the regular season games and in all the World Series games. He was to pay for that tense 1952 season physically and emotionally. It was inevitable.

16

The Last Hurrah

An extremely tired Phil Rizzuto landed in Lenox Hill Hospital in New York City very soon after the Yankees' 1952 World Series victory. He was physically exhausted, his blood pressure was low, and he was suffering from duodenal ulcers, a disorder not uncommon to people whose work is particularly tense, or who are themselves very tense.

On a bed next to Phil was Whitey Ford. He was in the hospital for a broken nose suffered in a game. It had bothered Whitey for some time. Now, after the Series, he was taking care of the injury.

"Great kid, this Whitey," said the Scooter, "but I miss those comic books Yogi reads when we room together."

When Yogi came to the Yankees, he was glad to see a familiar face. Yogi and Rizzuto knew each other when they were in the Navy. He asked to room with the Scooter, and they had roomed together in 1952 when the team was on the road.

There are so many stories about Yogi Berra that they could fill another book. For instance, when the fans gave him a Day in his home town, St. Louis, he responded to the honor in his

161

most humble manner, saying, "I want to thank you for making this night necessary." And when someone told him that he had seen the movie *Dr. Zhivago*, Berra asked, "What's wrong— are you sick?" There are thousands of such stories. Some of them aren't true, but rather the work of some comic inventing a so-called Berraism.

Berra and the Scooter got along very well as roomies except for one thing: Yogi never liked being alone, and he didn't like to sleep. He wanted to talk to Phil all night and would get angry when the Scooter shut off the lights. Whenever Phil went to bed early, Yogi, coming into the room, would turn on the lights and wake him up. When at last Yogi had to turn in himself, he insisted on hearing a bedtime story. In self-defense, just so he could get some sleep, the Scooter would calm the savage beast in Yogi by telling him the story of "The Three Little Pigs," "Snow White," or "Little Red Riding Hood."

Well, he didn't have to tell Whitey Ford any bedtime stories, but he had enough other concerns to occupy his mind.

There was the cyst on Phil's right arm.

"No," said his physician, Dr. Sidney Gaynor, to a reporter, "we don't plan to operate on the cyst. Right now there's nothing there to operate on. But he'll have to go on a diet for his ulcer."

Ulcer patients were generally put on a weight-reducing diet, but not Phil.

"This little man needs ten or twelve more pounds," the doctor continued. "We'll put him on a weight-*producing* diet."

But the rest in the hospital and the added weight weren't going to take the years off the Scooter. He had celebrated his thirty-fourth birthday, and there had been a lot of talk about the possibility of his retiring from the game.

When the question was put to Phil directly, he responded firmly, but quietly. "I read all about it in the papers. They've got me all washed up. Poor Phil, they say. He's over the hill. All through. A has-been.

"Well, this is nothing new to me. Some people have been washing me up as far back as I can remember.

"Luke Appling was forty years old and he played 142 games in 1949. Leo Durocher was two years older than I am before he quit as an active player. Frankie Frisch was thirty-eight when he played second base for that tough St. Louis Gas House Gang. Eddie Joost is two years older than I am and he's still playing a great game. And they tell me that Honus Wagner played 123 games the year he was forty-two.

"I'm not putting myself in a class with these guys," he concluded with his usual humility. "I'm just pointing out that infielders, and shortstops in particular, can last a long time."

Phil was sure he had a few more years left on the diamond.

"Who knows?" he said. "I may be able to go at top speed for another two years. For another three. Maybe just one more. There are such things as injuries.

"The way I figure this, I can play every day for three more seasons."

He was also beginning to think of what he might do once his playing days were over.

"After I'm finished as a regular, I would like to stay with the Yankees as a utility man, or a coach, or a manager somewhere."

Phil played, as he had predicted, in 1953, and he had a better bat that season, hitting .271, but there was no doubt that his play in the field was declining. Approaching his thirty-fifth birthday, he had lost something in his speed, something in his range. But he was still too good and meant too much to the team to be benched. He did bang up his right knee in June of that season and sat out for about a week, but he was back soon enough, helping the Yanks in their bid for yet another pennant.

His blood pressure fell, and in August he began taking pills to restore it to normal.

"The fact is," he explained, "I'm such a little guy that by August the daily play begins to tell on me. I don't have the old zip."

There was the old trouble with his eyes. He tried wearing glasses but they didn't help. But the Scooter hung in there, still the Yankee sparkplug, as Casey Stengel piloted the New York club to a record-breaking fifth straight American League flag. And Phil was in there, too, as Casey's Yanks set a new World Series record, beating the Dodgers again in the fall classic, this time four games to two, to bring New York its fifth straight world championship.

Little Phil got six hits in that Series for a beautiful batting average of .316. It was a great hurrah, but it was going to prove his last.

He still pooh-poohed the stories about his being washed up. He still protested that other baseball players, great baseball players, had starred in the game when they were older than he was. He still figured he had a couple of good years left.

"I'll be back in the spring," he stated. "You can count on it."

But Phil, for all his determination, was not unrealistic about his situation.

"Of course," he said, "when I say I'll be back next season it is not to say that I'll be in there for 154 games. I'll need more rest. It's been pretty tough for me in recent years, not being able to be benched because the pennants weren't clinched until very late.

"It got so I couldn't sleep. Or if I did sleep, I had nightmares. I dreamed that people were hemming me in and I couldn't get away. I'd wake up in the middle of the night in a cold sweat."

Yes, the Scooter's best days were behind him now. The years of the grueling wars on the diamond had taken their toll. Still, as he had predicted, he had a few years left.

In 1954 he played in 127 games and his play in the field, if it didn't sparkle as it had in his earlier years, was still good enough to keep him at shortstop for most of the season. But his bat fell off miserably. He wound up the year with his lowest average ever, .195, as the Yankees finished eight games behind the league-leading Cleveland Indians. It was the first time in six years that Stengel had failed to win the pennant.

In 1955, the Scooter played in only eighty-one games. Billy Hunter, acquired in a deal with the Baltimore Orioles, was the regular Yankee shortstop in 1955. It wasn't the happiest year for the Scooter. He had to be thinking of what the future, the very near future, held for him. He had dabbled a bit in radio, making occasional appearances on the air; he was half-owner of a clothing store in New York City and a bowling alley in Montclair, New Jersey, with Berra as his partner. But his heart and soul were in baseball. Where in baseball, after his playing days were over? That was the big question.

But it wasn't all sour for Phil in 1955. On Sunday, September 18, the fans turned out to honor the greatest shortstop the New York Yankees had ever boasted. It was Phil Rizzuto Day at Yankee Stadium.

"We in Hillside love you, Phil, as a neighbor, a wonderful

husband and father, and as a baseball player," said Henry Goldhor, mayor of Hillside, N.J., where the Rizzutos lived (and still reside), and honorary chairman of Rizzuto Day.

Jerry Coleman stepped to the microphone and handed Phil a silver tray. On it were inscribed the names of all the Yankee players, coaches, and manager Casey Stengel.

There were loads of other gifts for the Scooter, Cora, their three daughters, Patti, Cindy, and Penny, and for Phil's mother.

There was a huge television set, a freezer stocked with food and ice cream, china, glassware, silverware, cutlery. There were wardrobes of hats and slacks, luggage, a cocktail table, rugs, phonograph records, a wristwatch, a gold bracelet, fountain pens, and a year's supply of candy.

There was more. The original plan was to present the Scooter with an expensive car. It was Phil himself who vetoed that idea. Instead, the Scooter asked, in his typically generous manner, that the gift be presented to a worthwhile cause, and his request was granted. In place of the car, Phil was handed a check for $6,000. Today that amount would be worth close to $20,000. In turn, the Scooter handed back the check and asked that it be donated to the Phil Rizzuto Scholarship Fund. Phil established the fund to help needy high school graduates attend college.

Thanks to the fans and ballplayers, that fund was $2,000 richer before the end of Phil Rizzuto Day. Even the ushers chipped in, collecting a few hundred dollars among themselves.

Unassuming, humble Phil was overwhelmed by the outpouring of love. At the microphone, the lump in his throat was too big for him to talk, and the tears streamed from his eyes. All he could do was wave his hands at the fans, a gesture of his acknowledgment and thanks, and walk away, as the fans came near to breaking the sound barrier with their tumultuous applause.

It was a glorious day for the little guy, but even Phil knew, despite his attempts to drive the thought from his mind, that there were very few happy days left for him in a Yankee uniform.

17

On the Loose

Cora was worried about Phil in 1956. She thought it was time for the Scooter to call it quits on the baseball field and retire. On the other hand, she knew how much her husband loved the game, and she was concerned that leaving it might very well have a negative effect on his wonderful disposition, his good humor. She didn't quite know how to handle the situation, but she did the best she could.

"Phil won't quit for a long time," she said. "Last year and a few years ago, when he wasn't feeling too well, I thought I wanted him to retire. But the way he feels, I think he'd be the unhappiest man out of baseball. I won't let him be that."

Evidently Cora's feelings weren't clear to the Scooter.

"Cora and the kids have been after me for some time to quit," he said.

But certainly he had been thinking of quitting for some time, too, if not with any great determination.

"At first I used to get mad when they got after me to quit, but lately I've been considering it myself.

"I've been talking to Tommy Henrich and Joe DiMaggio and George Stirnweiss, asking them how it feels to be out of baseball. I'm beginning to realize it's not too bad. They're all happy. At least, they sound happy.

"They don't go home tense after a ballgame. They don't take any baseball worries home with them. They see their kids all the time. They tell me that they didn't think they'd like it, but it's great."

Seeing the kids was very, very important to the Scooter.

One morning, as Phil was getting ready to leave home for the ballpark, Cindy, who was about seven, turned to Phil and said, "You keep going away all the time. I'm going to get a daddy that stays home."

The sensitive Scooter choked on that.

"You hear your little kid say that, and it doesn't make you feel good. It's my fault. I've been away too much. Until I stopped making those winter appearances at banquets and dinners and all those other functions, the only time I had with my family was just before spring training when we go down to Florida."

The kids weren't the only ones who missed the Scooter.

"I get the blues when Phil goes away," Cora admitted. "The kids mention it an awful lot when he's not home, because he's such a good daddy to them."

Still, she wouldn't have him out of baseball until he was ready to leave on his own.

"I really believe Phil would be a lost soul if he gave up baseball. Baseball is his only interest."

On being happy, as DiMaggio and Stirnweiss and Henrich had reported it, Cora had a few wise words.

"Phil is so gullible. If they tell him they're happy being out of baseball, he believes them. Perhaps they are, but that doesn't mean it would be the same for Phil."

Still, Phil did have retirement on his mind and, for all the pain the thought of retiring from the diamond brought, he did some constructive planning for it.

There was his part-ownership of the clothing store and the bowling alley, and a few other investments.

"If I could make out in those businesses and be with my family, I think it would be great," the Scooter commented at the time.

In August 1956 he was considering the options open to him on retirement from baseball. It was likely, he thought, that some major league team would want him as manager.

"If the Giants or the Dodgers are interested," he said, the boyish twinkle in his eye, "I think they know where to reach me."

If not with the Giants or Dodgers, Phil felt with good reason that he had the makings of a good skipper. There weren't too many ballplayers, even coaches and managers, who knew the game as well as he did, and there were even fewer who could instill in others the spirit the Scooter brought to the game.

Then there was the offer to broadcast games for the Baltimore Orioles, but the Scooter didn't seriously consider that. Still, Phil knew he didn't have too many years left as a Yankee player.

"Why should they keep me in 1957?" he asked. "They've got Gil McDougald. He's the best shortstop in the business. And they've got Jerry Lumpe, Tony Kubek, and Bobby Richardson in the minors.

"I'll be talking to George Weiss soon. I'll lay all my cards on the table and we'll see what's what."

He sounded cheerful enough. He sounded ready enough for

that last day in his career as an active ballplayer. But when the axe fell, it came as a great shock to the Scooter, and to all New York Yankee fans as well. Perhaps it was how the axe fell that was so tough to take. After all, anyone with half an eye on the ball knew that sooner or later the Scooter would have to call it quits.

Late in August, with the pennant still up for grabs, the Yankees found themselves with just three outfielders, one of them a rookie. Bob Cerv, Irv Noren, Elston Howard, Joe Collins, and Norm Siebern were all injured or hurting and out of the lineup. The Yanks needed an outfielder desperately, and Enos Slaughter, the veteran left-handed slugger, then with Kansas City, was available. Kansas City had put him on waivers, and the last day to claim him was Saturday, the day before the Yankees' annual Old Timers game.

August 25 was Old Timers Day at the Stadium, and the old stars took the field to show their stuff before a full house. All the young timers on the Yankee club were out there, snapping away with their cameras at the greats of yesteryear. And the Scooter was out there, too, busy camera in hand, when he got a call to meet with Casey Stengel and George Weiss in Stengel's office in the Yankee clubhouse.

"Sit down," said Weiss, as the Scooter walked into the office.

Both Stengel and Weiss had some papers in front of them that they apparently had been studying before the Scooter's arrival.

"We're going over the roster," Weiss began. "Siebern and Noren are hurt, and we need another left-handed hitting outfielder for the World Series."

"Yeah?" said Phil with interest.

Weiss hesitated for a moment, then said quietly, "We want

to go over this list with you. We'll have to let somebody go to get the outfielder we want. We want your help to decide who it is we can most logically release."

If Phil had any concern about why he had been called in to meet with Casey and Weiss, it disappeared fast. He was being asked to help make a managerial decision, a front-office decision. It made him feel good, and he attacked the problem earnestly.

He read down the list on the Yankee roster, carefully, painstakingly.

"How about Charlie Silvera?" he suggested.

Charlie Silvera was a reserve catcher who rarely got into a game.

Weiss shook his head.

"No, not Silvera."

Another look down the list and Phil suggested Mickey McDermott.

"He doesn't pitch much," said the Scooter.

Again Weiss shook his head.

Phil suggested Rip Coleman, a young pitcher who didn't seem to be making it.

Weiss again said no.

The Scooter looked at George Weiss. Weiss had a poker face. He looked at Stengel. Casey turned his face away. Suddenly, Phil began to suspect the truth, began to understand why he had been called into this conference whose purpose was to cut a Yankee from the New York roster.

"Let's go over the list again," said Weiss.

The Scooter knew what was coming, but he wasn't ready to accept the inevitable, not just yet. He kept suggesting names and Weiss kept rejecting them.

After what must have seemed like an eternity to the Scooter, Weiss finally came out with what he had been thinking and planning all along.

"We've got McDougald, Coleman, and Billy Martin. They can all play shortstop."

He paused.

"Sure," said the Scooter. "They can all play shortstop."

Another moment of embarrassed silence.

"Phil," said Weiss, as gently as he could, "I'm afraid we'll have to let you go."

Phil didn't say a word. He couldn't. The tears had come into his eyes before George Weiss had begun his speech. Now they just flowed down his cheeks.

Without so much as a good-bye, he left the Yankee clubhouse and headed straight for his car in the parking lot, eager to get away as fast as he could. He particularly didn't want to see any of his teammates. He was just too upset to talk to anybody.

But he bumped into Jerry Coleman, who was coming off the field.

"Where are you going?" asked Jerry, surprised to see Phil leaving the Stadium.

"I've been given my release," said Phil flatly.

"Yeah, they just released me, too," said Coleman, joking.

Jerry just couldn't believe it. He was stunned when Phil convinced him that he wasn't kidding.

George Stirnweiss ran into Phil, too, and George tried to console him.

"It's going to hurt for a while," he said to the Scooter, "but you'll get over it. Just keep thinking that you've joined the club."

"What club?" asked Phil with some bitterness.

"You're in good company," George explained. "DiMaggio, Keller, Henrich, Lopat, Raschi, me, and all the other guys. It happened to all of us. Sooner or later we're through."

If this was supposed to make Phil feel better about his release, it didn't.

He heard the announcement of his release on the radio as he was driving. The report said something about Weiss offering him some kind of job in the Yankee organization.

At that moment, Phil wasn't interested. He had hoped to finish his playing days with the Yankees, and to announce his own retirement. He felt he had been given a raw deal.

The New York Yankee brass had terminated the career of one of its greatest players in a crass and ugly fashion. With no warning at all to the ballplayers or the fans the New York club had summarily dismissed the man who had sparked the team to ten American League pennants and eight world championships. Without any sense of responsibility to ballplayers or fans, without any sign of gratitude for what Phil had contributed to New York baseball, the front office had callously fired the Yankee ballplayer most loved by teammates and fans.

The fans raised the roof when the news about Phil Rizzuto reached them. The front office was besieged by phone calls, letters, and telegrams protesting the callous treatment of their hero. The Yankee front office found it necessary to defend itself, to try to explain its abrupt and unfeeling action.

They apologized for the suddenness of their action by disclosing that the deadline for the Slaughter deal was the day before the Old Timers game. They gave their plethora of shortstops as the reason for letting Rizzuto go. They also announced that Phil would be paid for the full season and share in the World Series revenues, and they revealed that the Scooter had earned $342,631 as a Yankee.

"He has earned it," the Yankee front office was gracious enough to say, "and the Yankees hope that he will go on to continued health, happiness, and success."

The front office also declared, "The Yankees feel that this lengthy explanation is necessary to set the record straight."

They had set the record straight, but the fans, and Phil Rizzuto, were not easily consoled.

When Phil got home the day he had been cut from the club, the silence hung like a dense cloud. The Scooter didn't have to say why he was home so early, and not at Yankee Stadium playing ball.

"I tried to get you on the phone," he began quietly.

"We heard," said Cora just as quietly, letting Phil know that he didn't have to go into details. "The children must have been in the backyard playing when you called."

Phil just sat down and said nothing for a while. His mind was reeling, his heart was heavy, and there wasn't anything he could say except that he was miserably unhappy, and he didn't want his children to hear that.

Cora, as unhappy as her husband, said nothing, afraid that anything she might say would only serve to deepen his despair.

The children, sensitive to the mood that enveloped the room, were quiet as well.

It was Phil who broke the heavy silence.

He took a baseball from his pocket and handed it to Penny.

"This is for you," he said to the kids.

It was a baseball, autographed by all the great ballplayers who had participated in the Old Timers Day at the Stadium.

Penny turned the ball around in her hands, reading off all

the names. When she finished, she turned to Phil and said with surprise, "Your name isn't on it, Daddy."

"No," said Phil.

"Why, Daddy?" Penny asked. "You're an old timer, aren't you?"

Cora stifled the gasp in her throat. Phil just smiled sadly.

"I'm not old enough to be an old timer," he said, his voice small, speaking more to himself than to the child, "and not young enough to be a Yankee."

Cora surreptitiously wiped the tears from her eyes.

It would be days, weeks, and months before the pall that descended on the Rizzuto home that unhappy day in late August 1956 would lift.

18

Holy Cow!

Frank Lane, general manager of the St. Louis Cardinals, got in touch with Phil just a day or two after the Scooter had been cut by the Yankees.

"We could use you," said Lane.

Phil was tempted.

"How about Alvin Dark?" he asked.

Alvin Dark, then with the Cards, was one of the top shortstops in the National League, but he wasn't as young as he used to be, either.

"He needs to be rested," explained Lane, "and you're the man to spell him."

The Scooter thought about it. There was nothing he would rather do than show the Yankee brass that he could still play the game and play it well.

But Phil was a man with strong loyalties. Perhaps the Yankees had been less than loyal to him, but it would be difficult for him to be disloyal to them, the only organization he had played for, in the minors and the majors, for so many years.

"If I sign with anybody," Phil told Frank Lane, "I'll sign

with you, but not as a player. My future," he added, "is not on
the field."

The Scooter had finally accepted the fact that his playing
days were behind him.

There were other possibilities in baseball, however. He
didn't give up the idea of managing in the big leagues, but
there was also the strong possibility of landing a job as a
broadcaster. Baltimore had previously offered him a three-
year contract to broadcast Oriole games. Phil had turned that
offer down because the job would take him away from his
family. Frankie Frisch, who broadcast the Giant games, asked
the Scooter to take over the postgame show for the New York
Giants at the Polo Grounds, and the Brooklyn Dodgers were
sounding him out about joining their broadcasting crew.

The Scooter wasn't a total stranger to broadcasting. In his
last couple of years with the Yankees, when Casey Stengel
occasionally took him out for a pinch hitter, Phil would change
quickly into his street clothes and make a beeline for the
broadcast booth. Mel Allen and Red Barber, who were doing
the games for the Yankees then, had an open invitation for the
Scooter, and they got him to do a half inning or so. Allen and
Barber got a kick out of it, but not nearly the kick the little
guy got.

"I loved it," said Phil. "Maybe it's the ham in me, but the
more I did it, the more I loved it."

And when the Yankees' front office offered him the job of
joining Mel Allen and Red Barber in the broadcast booth,
he jumped at it.

Maybe the Yanks were trying to make up for the crude way
they had released the Scooter from the club. Maybe they actually realized that Rizzuto would prove an asset to the Yankee

broadcast team. Whatever the motivation, they certainly made no mistake giving Phil the job. He has held the radio listeners and television viewers of the Yankee games glued to their sets for twenty-five years, from the day he started broadcasting in the spring of 1957.

Mel Allen and Red Barber were the best in the business. They took Phil in hand and taught him the ropes. They were great teachers and the Scooter learned quickly.

Phil began slowly, as Mel and Red coached him along. He would do the third inning on radio, the seventh on television. "It seemed like a breeze," Phil said. "Nothing to it."

The veteran broadcasters, however, soon taught the Scooter that broadcasting wasn't always as easy as it seemed, that sometimes the going could get rough.

It was the second week of spring training in 1957. The Yanks and the Cardinals were just about to begin their exhibition game when it began to rain. There wasn't much action to broadcast, not for a while anyway, until the rain let up.

"I'm going to get a hot dog with Red," Mel Allen told the Scooter, getting up from his chair. "We'll be right back. You take it."

The "it" was the radio microphone.

Phil couldn't say, "Hey, fellows, wait a minute! I've never done this kind of thing before." He had a job and he had to show he could do it. It was a kind of initiation for the Scooter —Mel knew it, and so did Phil. For the first time the Scooter was alone and faced with the most difficult task in broadcasting, filling dead air, amusing an audience when nothing is happening on the diamond.

For fifteen minutes, Mel and Red watched, out of sight from the Scooter, as Phil labored at the microphone, solo.

They could see him and hear him, as the Scooter filled the airways with a description of the field. But mostly he told stories about the players, how they felt about a rainy day, how they played the game, and so forth. It was a very, very long fifteen minutes for the Scooter, but he passed the test with flying colors.

"Not bad," said Red Barber, when the veterans returned to the booth.

"Pretty good," agreed Mel Allen.

Phil just sighed.

"You shouldn't have done that to me, fellows."

But the shock he had felt was soon gone, and Phil had reason to be pleased with himself. He had gone through his baptism by fire, and he had come through in fine shape. He wasn't going to worry anymore about performing solo on the radio, or on television either.

The Scooter had felt a bit peculiar at first about joining Allen and Barber in the broadcast booth.

"Here they were, two men who had passed the law bar," said Phil, "and me, I hadn't even graduated high school."

Mel and Red never pulled rank. They did, however, correct his English every now and then, and on the air.

"It's not 'pizza pie,' " Red Barber said, " 'Pizza' means pie."

"How was I to know?" protested the Scooter, who, though Italian through and through, confessed, "I'm not very strong with the Italian language."

"It's 'athletic,' not 'athaletic,' " said Mel Allen.

And Phil never took offense. Whenever he was corrected, he would say good-humoredly, "I didn't know that. Thanks."

There was a lot more Phil learned from the veteran broadcasters.

"The good broadcaster reacts to the play on the field before the crowd at the ballpark," says Phil. "He may not always be right, but at least he doesn't let the crowd lead him. He has to inform his audience, on the radio, or at the television, before the background noises of the fans at the game tip off his audience."

The Scooter gives Mel Allen credit for this piece of good advice.

"Mel could build up the drama of a play because he sensed that it was going to be tough but playable. And quite often, with a Yankee team that grabbed everything in sight, he was anticipating great plays."

But there were some of Allen's ideas that the Scooter didn't subscribe to.

"Mel was very superstitious. If a pitcher was working on a no-hitter, he would never mention it, afraid he would jinx it.

"Once I took over in the seventh and mentioned that Whitey Ford hadn't allowed a hit through six innings," recalled Rizzuto, "and Mel Allen almost jumped out of the booth.

" 'You just don't do that,' Allen yelled.

" 'But how is the audience supposed to know?' I asked. 'Suppose they tuned in late?'

" 'You just don't,' said Mel.

"And if a man was three for three in a game and up at bat for the fourth time, Mel wouldn't mention that the batter had had a perfect day until that moment. Mel had a lot of superstitions.

"But he was a perfectionist and he taught me a lot. If I said somebody hit a foul ball back, Mel would say, 'Back where? Tell them it's behind the plate, or behind first, or wherever.' "

Red Barber had another way of teaching the rookie broadcaster. He would ask Phil questions and get him to answer them.

"He knew the answers before I gave them," said the Scooter. "He just wanted the audience to hear them from me.

"There were times I might sense something he didn't. I remember seeing Billy Martin take a lead off third base and measure the pitcher for a steal home. I whispered to Red that it could happen right there. Well, instead of calling the play a possibility himself, Red said, 'Here, Phil, you take the mike.' And I came off smelling like roses."

Phil Rizzuto had two of the best teachers in the business to help him break into broadcasting, and with time the Scooter developed his own style. Nobody listening to Phil Rizzuto on the air could possibly mistake him for anyone else.

"Holy cow!"

"I don't believe this!"

"Oh! Did you see that!?"

These phrases are trademarks of the Scooter's enthusiastic personal style.

He is outspoken on the air. He doesn't conceal his emotions, going up and down with the fortunes of the Yankees.

He doesn't hesitate to take issue with an umpire when he believes the ump has made a bad call.

"That guy was safe! He slid right under the tag!"

He'll find fault with the official scorer from time to time, and let his audience know about it.

"He must have been looking somewhere else," is a typical Rizzuto reaction. "Maybe he had a bad angle on the play."

He'll just as soon find fault with the managerial strategy, or the way an infielder misplays a grounder.

"He's letting the ball play him. He should be playing the

ball," the Scooter will say, bringing his knowledge of the game to his play-by-play.

"Why did he play that ball barehanded? He didn't have to. He'll learn. He'll learn."

One of the Scooter's pet peeves is the way the official scorer often charges the catcher with an error, even if the error isn't legitimately his.

"That was a perfectly good throw he made to second. He would have had the runner nailed, if somebody had been there to catch it. It's not his fault that the ball wound up in center field. The second baseman and the shortstop got their signals crossed, or maybe they didn't have any signals. The second baseman or the shortstop should be charged with that error, not the catcher."

The Scooter speaks his mind on the microphone, and he doesn't pull any punches. But he is as quick to praise as he is to find fault—maybe quicker.

"Holy cow! I don't believe this! He reached over the fence to bring that ball in! Holy cow!" he will yell in praise as some outfielder makes an acrobatic catch.

He'll jump up and down in the broadcast booth with excitement.

"Unbelievable!" he will shout. "This is poetry in motion!"

Bill White, his considerably cooler partner at the mike these days, will say, rather calmly, "Yes. I'd have to say that was a five-star catch."

"Five?" says Phil, who doesn't go much for the star system of rating. "I'd give him six! Four for stopping the home run and two for the catch!"

As he was as a player, Phil Rizzuto is an enthusiastic broadcaster with a great sense of humor.

When Baltimore Oriole manager Earl Weaver threw a

fit during a game and got himself thumbed off the diamond, the Scooter remarked, "Weaver should get the Academy Award for that performance." Then, turning to Bill White, he said drily, "Don't you think Weaver ought to get seven stars for that act?"

Phil has been accused of being too one-sided in his work at the mike, that his loyalty to the Yankees colors his broadcasts; that he yells loudest when a Yankee makes a good play or gets a hit; that he doesn't give the opposition players the credit they deserve for their batting or fielding; that he is cheerful as all get out when the Yankees are winning, and down in the mouth when the Yankees are losing.

Phil has a simple answer.

"I'm a Yankee fan first, a broadcaster second."

Fortunately for the Scooter, the Yankees these days are a winning ballclub. He does tense up when the New Yorkers aren't doing what he'd like them to do—win. In most games he banters a lot with the other broadcasters. He'll talk about anything from Cora to the kids, from old movies to what he had for dinner the night before, from some funny story about Yogi Berra to some hilarious incident in his minor league days. On occasion he'll say something that just doesn't make much sense at all.

"The cream always rises to the top," he declared once, when the going on the field was slow.

Fran Healy, who handled the color commentary on the radio for the Yankees through the 1981 season, was the straight man for this one.

"Who told you that?" he demanded of the Scooter.

"My milkman," responded Phil in a dead-pan tone that any comedian would envy.

It was the kind of talk that made listeners laugh—or grimace, for Phil has his critics as well as his army of supporters. He has never really tried to be a comedian. He just has a good time up there in the booth. Nobody enjoys his work more than Phil enjoys broadcasting those Yankee games.

"I certainly do enjoy my job," Phil says. "It's almost like stealing, to get paid for something you enjoy so much."

He'll tell that to anybody and everybody but, if it's a sportswriter he is talking to, he'll add, "Be sure you make that *almost*, almost like stealing." And he'll flash a big grin.

Mel Allen was let go by the Yankees after the 1964 season. Red Barber was released. Joe Garagiola, who had played as a catcher with the St. Louis Cardinals and three other National League teams, joined Phil for a while in the Yankee broadcast booth. Jerry Coleman, the star Yankee second baseman, worked with Phil for a while before he departed, too. Phil has remained the voice of the Yankees for twenty-five years. Bill White and Frank Messer have been his broadcast partners for a number of years, and in 1982 he was joined by John Gordon, who replaced Fran Healy.

Phil has done other work on radio and TV. His daily show on CBS radio, "It's Sports Time," ran for more than fifteen years. He has been a guest star on many TV shows, and he still does commercials for The Money Store and other concerns.

Phil turned sixty-four in 1982. For a few years there has been some talk of his retiring, the latest flap coming on July 27, 1982, when a *New York Post* headline blared HOLY COW! SCOOTER IS CALLING IT QUITS. However, that night during the Yankee broadcast, Phil declared that he would continue his stint in the booth as long as the game of baseball gave him a thrill—presumably forever. "They'll have to carry me out of Yankee Stadium," he quipped to Frank Messer.

Phil does have one great ambition left in baseball. He

doesn't talk about it much, but when the subject comes up, a starry look enters his eyes. He would like to be beside teammates such as Joe DiMaggio, Lefty Gomez, Red Ruffing, Mickey Mantle, Yogi Berra, Whitey Ford, and Casey Stengel in the Baseball Hall of Fame in Cooperstown, New York. It is an honor he richly deserves for the invaluable contribution he made to the Yankee dynasty of the 1940s and '50s.

Phil Rizzuto has been in baseball, on the field or at the mike, for forty-six years, and that's not counting the years he played ball in school and on the sandlots of Brooklyn. There are few men alive today who have been involved with the game as long as Phil.

Cora has said, "I don't know what Phil will do if he isn't around baseball."

No one else knows, either. It's impossible to think of Phil Rizzuto without baseball or baseball without Phil Rizzuto.

APPENDIX A: THE SCOOTER'S LIFETIME STATS

Year	Club	G	AB	R	H	2B	3B	HR	RBI	BB	SO	SB	BA	PO	A	E	FA
						Minor and Major Leagues											
1937	Bassett	67	284	53	88	17	5	5	NA	NA	NA	NA	.310	162	217	27	.933
1938	Norfolk	112	446	97	150	24	10	9	58	NA	NA	NA	.336	169	376	36	.938
1939	Kansas City	135	503	99	159	21	6	5	64	NA	NA	NA	.316	244	394	38	.944
1940	Kansas City	148	579	124	201	28	10	10	73	NA	NA	35	.347	325*	515*	45	.949
1941	NY Yankees	133	515	65	158	20	9	3	46	27	36	14	.307	252	399	29	.957
1942	NY Yankees	144	553	79	157	24	7	4	68	44	40	22	.284	324*	445	30	.962
1943–45							Military Service										
1946	NY Yankees	126	471	53	121	17	1	2	38	34	39	14	.257	267	378	26	.961
1947	NY Yankees	153	549	78	150	26	9	2	60	57	31	11	.273	340	450	25	.969
1948	NY Yankees	128	464	65	117	13	2	6	50	60	24	6	.252	259	348	17	.973
1949	NY Yankees	153	614	110	169	22	7	5	64	72	34	18	.275	329	440	23	.971*
1950	NY Yankees	155	617	125	200	36	7	7	66	91	38	12	.324	301*	452	14	.982*
1951	NY Yankees	144	540	87	148	21	6	2	43	58	27	18	.274	317	407	24	.968
1952	NY Yankees	152	578	89	147	24	10	2	43	67	42	17	.254	308	458*	19	.976
1953	NY Yankees	134	413	54	112	21	3	2	54	71	39	4	.271	214	409	24	.963
1954	NY Yankees	127	307	47	60	11	0	1	15	41	23	3	.195	185	294	16	.968
1955	NY Yankees	81	143	19	37	4	1	0	9	22	18	7	.259	93	132	10	.957
1956	NY Yankees	31	52	6	12	0	0	0	6	6	6	3	.231	31	54	6	.934
Major League Totals		1661	5816	877	1588	239	62	38	562	650	397	149	.273	3220	4666	263	.968

(Continued)

APPENDIX A: THE SCOOTER'S LIFETIME STATS (Cont.)

Year	Club	G	AB	R	H	2B	3B	HR	RBI	BB	SO	SB	BA	PO	A	E	FA
								World Series									
1941	NY Yankees	5	18	0	2	0	0	0	0	3	1	1	.111	12	18	1	.968
1942	NY Yankees	5	21	2	8	0	0	1	1	2	1	2	.381	15	14	1	.967
1947	NY Yankees	7	26	3	8	1	0	0	2	4	0	2	.308	19	15	0	1.000
1949	NY Yankees	5	18	2	3	0	0	0	1	3	1	1	.167	5	15	0	1.000
1950	NY Yankees	4	14	1	2	0	0	0	1	3	0	1	.143	5	8	0	1.000
1951	NY Yankees	6	25	5	8	1	0	1	3	2	3	1	.320	14	23	1	.974
1952	NY Yankees	7	27	2	4	1	0	0	0	5	2	0	.148	13	17	1	.968
1953	NY Yankees	6	19	4	6	1	0	0	0	3	2	1	.316	11	19	1	.968
1955	NY Yankees	7	15	2	4	0	0	0	1	5	1	2	.267	13	14	0	1.000
Totals		52	183	21	45	3	0	2	8	30	11	10	.246	107	143	5	.980
								All Star Games									
1950	American		6	0	2	0	0	0	0	0		0	.333	2	2	0	1.000
1951	American		1	0	0	0	0	0	0	0		0	.000	1	2	0	1.000
1952	American		2	0	0	0	0	0	0	0		0	.000	1	0	0	1.000
1953	American		0	0	0	0	0	0	0	0		0	.000	1	0	0	1.000
Totals			9	0	2	0	0	0	0	0		0	.222	5	4	0	1.000

Key: * = league leader among shortstops; NA = not available; G = games; AB = at bats; R = runs; H = hits; 2B = doubles; 3B = triples; HR = home runs; RBI = runs batted in; BB = bases on balls; SO = strikeouts; SB = stolen bases; BA = batting average; PO = put outs; A = assists; E = errors; FA = fielding average.

Note. In World Series play, Phil Rizzuto is among the lifetime leaders in several categories: games (6th), at bats (7th), hits (tied for 7th), runs (tied for 10th), bases on balls (4th), and stolen bases (tied for 3rd).

APPENDIX B: HALL OF FAME SHORTSTOPS AND THE SCOOTER—A COMPARISON

Every Phil Rizzuto fan firmly believes that the Scooter deserves a place in the Hall of Fame. Indeed, after the Veteran's Committee made its selection in 1982, the first year that Rizzuto was eligible to be inducted by that group (the Veteran's Committee makes its selection from players who have been retired for at least 25 years), and Rizzuto was *not* chosen, a New York daily newspaper reported indignantly SCOOTER SNUBBED.

Following is a list of Hall of Famers who played most of their games at shortstop, along with some statistics. Admittedly, as Lollypop Corriden is quoted as saying about the Scooter on page 113, "His value can't be measured by mere fielding and batting averages. It's something that goes deeper," and this is true of all the men listed below. However, despite their limitations, these stats should be good for settling some arguments, and perhaps starting a few more, regarding the Scooter's claim on Cooperstown.

	Years Played	G	AB	H	HR	R	RBI	BB	SO	BA	SB	FA
Luke Appling	1930–1950	2422	8857	2479	45	1319	1116	1302	528	.310	179	.948
Dave Bancroft	1915–1930	1913	7182	2004	32	1048	591	827	487	.279	145	.944
Lou Boudreau	1938–1952	1646	6030	1779	68	861	789	796	309	.295	51	.973
Joe Cronin	1926–1945	2124	7579	2285	170	1233	1424	1059	700	.301	87	.953
Travis Jackson	1922–1936	1656	6086	1768	135	833	929	412	565	.291	71	.951
Hugh Jennings	1891–1918	1285	4904	1527	18	994	840	347	117	.311	359	.946
Rabbit Maranville	1912–1935	2670	10078	2605	28	1255	884	839	756	.258	291	.956
Joe Sewell	1920–1933	1902	7132	2226	49	1141	1051	844	114	.312	74	.954
Joe Tinker	1902–1916	1804	6439	1694	31	774	782	416	114	.263	336	.937
Honus Wagner	1897–1917	2789	10449	3430	101	1740	1732	963	327	.328	722	.946
Bobby Wallace	1894–1918	2386	8662	2324	35	1057	1121	774	79	.268	201	.940
Monte Ward*	1878–1894	1825	7647	2123	26	1408	686	420	326	.278	504	.905
Phil Rizzuto	1941–1956	1661	5816	1588	38	877	562	650	397	.273	149	.968

Key: * = also pitched 2461.2 innings, winning 158 games, losing 102; G = games; AB = at bats; H = hits; HR = home runs; R = runs; RBI = runs batted in; BB = bases on balls; SO = strikeouts; BA = batting average; SB = stolen bases; FA = fielding average.
Note: Statistics are for regular-season play only. Fielding average is figure for all positions played during career.

Index